The
Uncertainties
of Knowledge

In the series

Politics, History, and Social Change

edited by John Torpey

The
Uncertainties
of Knowledge

Immanuel Wallerstein

Temple University Press
PHILADELPHIA

Temple University Press, Philadelphia 19122
Copyright © 2004 by Temple University
Published 2004
Printed in the United States of America

⊗ The paper used in this publication meets the requirements of the
American National Standard for Information Sciences—Permanence
of Paper for Printed Library Materials, ANSI Z39.48–1984

Library of Congress Cataloging-in-Publication Data

Wallerstein, Immanuel Maurice, 1930–
      The uncertainties of knowledge / Immanuel Wallerstein.
          p.   cm. — (Politics, history, and social change)
      Includes bibliographical references and index.
      ISBN 1-59213-242-1 (cloth : alk. paper) — ISBN 1-59213-243-X
  (pbk. : alk. paper)
      1. Social sciences—Philosophy.   2. Scientism.   3. Education,
  Higher—Social aspects.   4. Social change.   I. Title.   II. Series.

  H61.15.W35 2004
  300'.1–dc22   2003061649

2   4   6   8   9   7   5   3   1

To the memory of Ilya Prigogine (1917–2003)
Scientist, Humanist, Scholar

Contents

The
Uncertainties
of Knowledge

Introduction
The Uncertainties of Time

Time in most ways seems so certain to us. These days, almost everyone has a watch and can measure the time that is passing. Yet nothing is in fact more uncertain than time. It is not quite a social illusion, but it is very nearly so. Consider this.

We all live in the present. Most of us think we know, or know best, what is happening now, at least in our immediate environs. Yet the present is the most evanescent of realities. The present is over the nanosecond it occurs. It cannot be recaptured. It can be recorded at most ultra-partially. It is remembered badly. Its memory and its records can easily be faked. It is rare that two eyewitnesses to the same event observe it in the same way, and rarer still that they remember it in the same way.

And yet we live in the present and are constantly making decisions, acting singly and collectively, to affect the present. Probably nothing matters to most of us as much as the present. In order to make these decisions in the present, singly and collectively, we invoke the past. But what is the past? In reality, the past is what we in the present think it is. No doubt there is a real past, but we can only know it in the present, through whatever lens we wish to apply to it. And of course, as a result, we all see different pasts. We see different pasts as individuals, we see different pasts as groups, we see different pasts as scholars.

Not only do we see different pasts, but it is terribly important to all of us that we impose our vision of the past on everyone else. It is terribly important because the modal images of the past at any moment are a determining element in the actions of the present at that moment. Furthermore, our modal images of the past are not stable. They change constantly, almost as rapidly as the present. This is because our actions in the present require that the past be reinterpreted. The politics of the present is insistent and persistent in this regard. Governments argue about the past, social movements argue about the past, scholars argue about the past. Nor are these arguments gentle dispassionate debates. On the contrary, these debates are ferocious, often angry, sometimes death-dealing. And they are never resolved. The most that happens is that a wide consensus is temporarily built, a consensus that always has dissenters and that lasts as long as it lasts in the places in which it takes hold.

Well then, what of the future? Faced with the ephemeral nature of the present, and the ever-changing nature of the past, many flee into the future and seek certainty there. The basis of this certainty about the future can be theological or political or scientific. But since the future has not yet happened, it can never be ascertained whether these predictions are in fact correct. Predictions that involve specific short-term statements have been regularly shown not to hold, or not to hold precisely. And eschatologies are intrinsically unverifiable. Faith in the future has varied over historical time. It was unusually strong in the nineteenth and twentieth centuries. But at the end of that period, a wave of disillusionment swept the globe, and large numbers of people lost this faith. Still, there always remain some who invest in the certainties of the future.

So here we are. We cannot know the present, we cannot know the past, we cannot know the future. Where does that leave us, and in particular where does it leave social science, which is devoted presumably to explaining social reality? In great difficulty, I should think. We are not, however, without resources. If we take uncertainty as a basic building block of our systems of knowledge, we may perhaps be able to construct understandings of reality that, albeit inherently approximate and certainly not deterministic, will be useful heuristically in focusing us on the historical options we have in the present in which we all live.

This book is an attempt to explore the parameters of such uncertain knowledge, and to suggest what might be done to enhance its value and make it more relevant to our individual and collective needs, passions, and hopes. Science is an adventure and an opportunity for us all, and we are called to participate in it, to build it, and to know its limitations.

PART I

The Structures of Knowledge

1 For Science, Against Scientism

The Dilemmas of Contemporary Knowledge Production

Science is under attack these days. It no longer enjoys the uncontested esteem it has had for two centuries as the most certain form of truth—for many, the only certain form of truth. We had become accustomed to believe that because theology, philosophy, and folk wisdom were all contestable as claims to truth, only science could offer certainty. The very modesty of the scientists' claims—all scientific assertions are subject to revision if and when new data become available—seemed to distinguish it from these rival forms of truth assertion, which scientists asserted to be ideological or speculative or traditional or subjective, hence less (even far less) reliable. For very many, the label "scientific" and the label "modern" became virtually synonymous, and for almost everyone the label was meritorious.

In the past twenty years, however, science has come under the identical form of attack to which the scientists had long subjected theology, philosophy, and folk wisdom. Now science too is being accused of being ideological, subjective, and unreliable. It has been argued that one can discern in

the theorizing of scientists many *a priori* premises that ultimately reflect nothing but currently dominant cultural
views. It has been argued that scientists manipulate data
and then manipulate the credibility of the public audience.
To the degree that these charges can be sustained, they
would of course merely be subjecting scientists to the same
kinds of critical cultural judgment to which scientists have
subjected all others.

Some critics, however, have gone further. They have
made the case for the nonexistence of universal truth, for
the necessary subjectivity of all knowledge assertions. The
response of the scientists to this stronger criticism, this expression of total relativism, has been to denounce such attacks
as the return of irrationalism. Some scientists have gone still
further and have asserted that even the moderate criticisms
of science, based on an analysis of the social embeddedness
of scientific activity, have been nefarious, in that they have
provided the entry onto the slippery slope that leads eventually to nihilistic relativism.

Culturally, this is where we are today worldwide. We
find ourselves in a conflict of mutual name calling in the
ongoing struggle for the control of resources and of institutions of knowledge. It is time we took stock and reflected on
the philosophical premises of our scientific activity and the
political context of the structures of knowledge.

How do we know that a new scientific claim is valid or
even plausible? Amid the reality of an ever increasing degree
of complex specialization of knowledge, for each specific scientific allegation, all but a very small number of persons are
bereft of a capacity for individual rational judgment either
about the quality of the evidence proffered or about the
tightness of the theoretical reasoning applied to the analysis of the data. The "harder" the science, the truer this is. If,

therefore, any of us reads in a general scientific journal, say, *Nature*, or in a sophisticated newspaper, say, the *Times of India*, that scientist X puts forward a claim to new knowledge, what leads us to credit it as reasonable? We tend to use the criteria of cumulative attestation by reputed authority. We rank loci of publication of the news on a reliability scale. We do the same with the people who make comments on the new proposition. Where do we get such reliability scales for the testimony of the journals or the quoted scholars? Such scales seldom exist in written form. Hence we in fact get these reliability scales from further reliability scales. If other "serious" people we know say that *Nature* is a prestigious, reliable journal, then we generally believe that it is. It is easy to see how much such implicit reliability scales build on each other.

What keeps them from crumbling like houses of cards? We rely on the likelihood that the multiple "experts" in any given narrow domain of knowledge will keep a close eye on each other and will speak up loudly and publicly if the quality of the data is poor or the quality of the reasoning is thin, or if contrary evidence is neglected, or *a fortiori* if there is actual fraud. Thus quiescence among the relevant experts is taken to be consent, and this consensus reassures us and allows us to incorporate new truths into our personal knowledge-storage system, whereas disputation arouses skepticism in us about the truth claim. This means that we do not defer to single experts but rather to self-constituted communities of experts.

But what makes us believe that a community of experts that speaks more or less with a single voice merits our respect and our credence? We give them respect and credence largely on the basis of two assumptions: they are well trained by creditable institutions, and they are reasonably disinterested. It is as a pair that we value these criteria. We assume that specialized knowledge is difficult to acquire, demanding long and rigorous apprenticeship. We put our faith in formal institutions, which in turn are evaluated by reliability scales. We assume that comparable institutions check each other, and thus that worldwide mutual evaluations ensure the reliability of such explicit and implicit scales. In short, we trust that professionals have appropriate skills, and most particularly the skill to evaluate new truth claims in their fields. We credit credentials and reputations.

In conjunction with our faith in credentials, we trust the relative disinterestedness of the scientists. We believe that scientists (unlike, once again, theologians, philosophers, and purveyors of folk wisdom) are psychically ready to accept any truth that emerges from an intelligent reading of the data, without feeling the need to hide these truths or to distort them or deny them.

It is precisely these claims to a combination of good training and disinterestedness upon which the skeptics of the past twenty years have focused. On the one hand, they have argued that professional training has often, perhaps almost always, been so organized as to omit important elements in their analyses or to distort such elements. This is only in part a function of the social bases of recruitment of scientists. To be sure, to the extent that scientists are disproportionately drawn from socially dominant strata worldwide, it may be thought that the selection of problems may suffer distortion. This seems quite evident for the social sciences but appears to have been true for the physical sciences as well. Even more important has been the choice of theoretical premises, the use of defining metaphors. Here the scientific bias has been less visible, more deeply buried. This has led the critics to go beyond the question of deliberate bias (prejudice) to the question of structural or institutionalized bias (of which the scientist may be unaware). If all this were true, then the training would have been inadequate, even possibly negative.

Of course, it is not merely a question of training but of norms. The norm of disinterestedness is central to the institutionalization of modern science. Even if this norm is violated by one or another scientist, it is presumed that the norm is sufficiently strong as to constrain the tendencies to violate it. Disinterestedness presumably means that the scientist will pursue enquiry where the logic of his analysis and the patterns of his data lead, and will be ready to make public the results even if such publication could damage some social policy the scientist supports or the reputations of colleagues he admires. The very concept of disinterestedness presumes an unhesitating choice by the scientist for honesty rather than dishonesty. But of course in the real world it doesn't work like that. Scientists are subject to many pressures: external ones from governments, influential institutions or persons, peers, internal ones from his or her superego. We all, without exception, respond to such pressures up to a point. Furthermore, there is the Heisenberg principle writ large. The process of investigation, the procedure through which the observations are made, transforms the object of investigation. Under certain circumstances, it transforms it so much that the data obtained are quite unreliable.

Furthermore, the self-interest of the scientific corporation may impinge on the training program. The system of professional certification of professionals, justified on the basis of preserving disinterestedness, permits the corporation to limit entry into the profession globally for motives that are extraneous to, even antagonistic to, the principle of disinterestedness. Yet political intrusion into the process of certification (the opposite of the corporate autonomy of professionals) may do the same thing. It seems to be Scylla and Charybdis.

But if competent training and disinterestedness erode as guarantees under close scrutiny, on what basis can we rely upon the pronouncements of experts? And if we cannot rely on such pronouncements, how can we ever accept the validity of scientific claims, at least in all those fields about which we claim no direct competence?

There is one strong answer to such acute skepticism. If we do not rely upon specialists, how can we ever know about most things? From what other source can we derive more reliable judgments? Will we in fact do better if we reject all specialists on the ground that their claims to authority are in fact specious? We can translate this into a major practical issue that most of us face regularly: maintaining our health. On the one hand, modern science tells us that living organisms may malfunction, "become ill." It also tells us that, in many situations, medical interventions may repair the malfunctioning. It further tells us that, in many cases, absent such intervention, we shall "get worse," even die. On the other hand, we know that contemporary doctors disagree on diagnoses, on prognoses, and on treatments. Furthermore, we know there have been disagreements over time (the prescriptions of 1990 are quite different from those of 1890) and, to some extent, over space. And we know there are iatrogenic maladies.

If we have a high fever, we may seek advice and assistance. If we are not ready to take it from the physician-scientist, from whom are we ready to take it, and on what grounds? Obviously, it makes a difference how serious a medical intervention is recommended. Treatment by aspirin is most often viewed casually. Recommendation of complicated brain surgery makes patients hesitate. In the end, most of us follow someone's advice on complicated brain surgery, *faute de mieux,* but whose? We hesitate to agree; we hesitate even more to bet on our skepticism.

Ergo what? It seems to me clear that we should not throw out the baby with the bath water. That is why I am using the title "For Science, Against Scientism." By scientism I mean the claim that science is disinterested and extrasocial, that its truth claims are self-sustaining without reference to more general philosophical assertions, and that science represents the only legitimate mode of knowledge. It seems to me that the skeptics of recent years, in many cases simply reviving ancient critiques, have shown the logical weakness of scientism. Insofar as scientists defensively protect scientism, they will delegitimize science.

Science by contrast seems to me an essential human adventure, perhaps indeed the great human adventure. Science seems to me to consist of two relatively modest but absolutely crucial claims: (1) There is a world outside and beyond the perception of any one of us that has existed and will exist. This world is not a fantasy of our mind. With this claim, we refuse a solipsistic view of the universe. (2) This real world is *partially* knowable empirically, allowing us to summarize this knowledge in heuristic theorizing. Even though it is intrinsically impossible ever to know the world entirely and completely, and certainly ever to predict the future correctly (since the future is not determined), it is eminently useful to seek to learn what we can in order to interpret reality better and to improve the conditions of our existence. Since, however, the reality of the world is ever changing, all such interpretations are necessarily transitory, and we would do well to be prudent in the conclusions we draw about practical matters. The situation we all recognize ourselves to be in vis-à-vis medical advice may be the eternal human condition. We can never be sure of the experts, but it's unlikely we shall do much better by dispensing with them.

We are faced with all sorts of decisions, small and great. Improving the capacities of a computer, for example, is a small decision, however large in scope the consequences. It may perhaps be relatively safe for all of us collectively to allow engineers considerable free rein in this process of technological improvement, and largely to trust in their expertise. Even here, we shall of course want to subject their narrow technical decisions to larger social concerns (does the new technology adversely affect our health or the environment or public safety?), questions that are not the specialty or even perhaps the concern of the computer engineer. Constructing a world order, on the other hand, is a large decision, complex, and for most of us seemingly remote from our immediate capacities to act. The level of disinterestedness of the presumed experts (politicians or scholars) is doubtless quite low. The meaningfulness of credentials is dubious. (How much good advice have the collectivity of economists given us about public policy on the economy lately?) And yet this may be a far more urgent and important issue than improving the capacities of a computer.

What is more, most people are aware of this. Faced with this urgency, many people worldwide have turned from scientistic claims to knowledge to claims based on theology, philosophy, or folk wisdom. Are we sure such alternate claims are less reliable? If so, on what basis are we so sure? This is indeed the challenge of contemporary knowledge production.

This is not the place to review the critical juncture of our contemporary world-system, something I have done often elsewhere. Let me merely assert that we are at one. The question is whether we can offer scientific analyses that are not scientistic about the historical choices before us. No doubt much underbrush must first be removed if we are to succeed. The heavy hand of scientism is part of what needs to be removed. We need to recognize that scientific choices are informed by values and intent as much as by knowledge of efficient causes. We need to incorporate utopistics into the social sciences. We need to move from an image of the neutral scientist to that of the intelligently concerned scientist restrained in the exercise of his hybris.

2 Social Sciences in the Twenty-first Century

To write about what will, or even may, occur is always hazardous. It involves an irreducible element of speculation because the future is intrinsically uncertain (Prigogine 1997). What one can do is try to ascertain the trends of the recent past, the possible continuing trajectories, and the loci of possible social choice. Inevitably this means arguing how the social sciences have been historically constructed, what are the current challenges to these constructs, and what are the consequent plausible alternatives of the coming decades and century.

There is a second difficulty about discussing the future of the social sciences. The social sciences are not a bounded, autonomous arena of social action. They are a segment of a larger reality, the structures of knowledge of the modern world. Furthermore, they have been largely, albeit not entirely, located within a major institutional framework of the modern world, the world university system. It is hard to discuss the historical construction of the social sciences, the current challenges, or the existing plausible alternatives without placing the social sciences within the evolution of the structures of knowledge as a whole and within the evolving institutional framework of the university system.

I shall therefore address these issues in three time frames—the historical construction, the present challenges, and the plausible future alternatives. I shall deal with the first two time frames in broad brushstrokes, simply to provide the background for the discussion of the future. Within each time framework, I shall treat three things—the structures of knowledge as a whole, the evolution of the university system, and the particular character of the social sciences.

The structures of knowledge of the modern world are quite different from those known in any previous world-system in one fundamental way. In all other historical systems, whatever their value systems and in whichever group within them the primary responsibility for the production and reproduction of knowledge was placed, all knowledge was considered to be epistemologically unified. Of course, there may have developed many different schools of thought within any given historical system, and there may have been many struggles over the content of "truth," but it was never considered that there were two radically different kinds of truth. The unique feature of the modern world-system is that it developed a structure of knowledge within which there are "two cultures," to use the now famous phrase of C. P. Snow (1965).

The historical construction of the social sciences occurred within the tense framework that was created by the existence of "two cultures." But the two cultures first had to be created themselves.[1] The absence of boundaries was double. There was little sense that scholars had to confine their activities to one field of knowledge. And there was certainly almost no sense that philosophy and science were distinct arenas of knowledge. This situation was to change radically sometime between 1750 and 1850, resulting in the so-called "divorce" between science and philosophy. We have ever since been operating within a structure of knowledge in which "philosophy" and "science" have been considered distinctive, indeed virtually antagonistic, forms of knowledge.

The emergence of this new structure of knowledge, the epistemological divide between science and philosophy, was reflected in the university system in two important ways. The first was the reorganization of the faculties. The medieval European university had had four faculties: theology (the most important), medicine, law, and philosophy. Beginning in 1500 theology became less important, and it nearly disappeared by the nineteenth century. Medicine and law became more narrowly technical. It is the evolution of the faculty of philosophy, however, that was the crucial story.

Two things happened to the faculty of philosophy. First, in the eighteenth century, new institutions of higher learning emerged inside and outside it that were "specialized."[2] The university system was able to survive essentially by creating within the faculty of philosophy the series of specializations we today call disciplines, and by assembling these disciplines no longer within a single faculty of philosophy but usually within two separate ones, a faculty of arts (or humanities or philosophy) and a faculty of sciences.

Second, what is significant about this organic restructuring is not only the institutionalization of a division between philosophy and science but the steady rise of the cultural prestige of science at the expense of the humanities/ philosophy. In the beginning, the sciences had to fight for their preeminence and initially found the university system somewhat hostile,[3] but soon the balance was reversed.

Where, then, did social science fit in this picture? Social science was institutionalized only in the late nineteenth century, and in the shadow of the cultural dominance of Newtonian science. Faced with the claims of the "two cultures," the social sciences internalized their struggle as a

Methodenstreit. There were those who leaned toward the humanities and used what was called an idiographic epistemology. They emphasized the particularity of all social phenomena, the limited utility of all generalizations, and the need for empathetic understanding. And there were those who leaned toward the natural sciences and used what was called a nomothetic epistemology. They emphasized the logical parallel between human processes and all other material processes. They sought therefore to join physics in the search for simple universal laws that held true across time and space. Social science was like someone tied to two horses galloping in opposite directions. Having developed no epistemological stance of its own, social science was torn apart by the struggle between the two colossi that were the natural sciences and the humanities, neither of which tolerated a neutral stance.

I shall not review here the internal methodological struggles of the social sciences, as they sought to carve a space for themselves amid the two-culture split between science and the humanities. Suffice it to remember that, in this *Methodenstreit*, the three principal disciplines that were created to deal with the modern world—economics, political science, and sociology—all opted to be nomothetic, by which they meant replicating to the extent possible the methods and epistemological worldview of Newtonian mechanics. The other social sciences thought of themselves as more humanistic and narrative but nonetheless attempted in their own partial manner to be "scientific." The humanistic scholars embraced the scientific emphasis on empirical data but caviled at the idea of universal "generalizations."

The "disciplinarization" of the social sciences, as a domain of knowledge "in between" the humanities and the natural sciences and profoundly split between the "two cultures," reached a point of clarity and simplicity by 1945. Initially, from 1750 to 1850, the situation had been very confused. Many, many names were used as the appellations of proto-disciplines, and none or few of them seemed to command wide support. Then, in the period from 1850 to 1945, this multiplicity of names was effectively reduced to a small, standard group clearly distinguished the one from the others. In our view, there were only six such names that were very widely accepted throughout the scholarly world, and they reflected three underlying cleavages that seemed plausible in the late nineteenth century: the split between past (history) and present (economics, political science, and sociology); the split between the Western civilized world (the above four disciplines) and the rest of the world (anthropology for "primitive" peoples and Oriental studies for non-Western "high civilizations"); and the split, valid only for the modern Western world, between the logic of the market (economics), the state (political science), and civil society (sociology).

After 1945 this clear structure began to break down for several reasons. The rise of area studies led to the incursion of the West-oriented disciplines into the study of the rest of the world and undermined the function of anthropology and Oriental studies as the special disciplines for these areas (Wallerstein 1997b). The worldwide expansion of the university system led to a considerable expansion of the number of social scientists. The consequent search for niches led to much "poaching" across previous disciplinary boundaries and hence to considerable de facto blurring of the disciplinary boundaries. Subsequently, in the 1970s, the demand for academic inclusion of previously ignored groups (women, "minorities," non-mainstream social groups) led to the creation of new interdisciplinary programs of study in the universities. All of this meant that the number of legitimate names of fields of study has started to expand, and there is every sign that this number will continue to grow. Given the erosion of disciplinary boundaries and de facto overlap, and the expansion of fields, we are in a sense moving back in the direction of the situation of 1750 to 1850, in which there were quite a large number of categories that did not provide a useful taxonomy.

The social sciences have also been affected by the fact that the trimodal division of knowledge into the natural sciences, the humanities, and the social sciences has come under attack. There have been two main new knowledge movements involved, and neither of them originated from within the social sciences. One is what has come to be called "complexity studies" (originating in the natural sciences) and the other "cultural studies" (originating in the humanities). In reality, starting from quite different standpoints, both of these movements have taken as their target of attack the same object, the dominant mode of natural science since the seventeenth century, that is, that form of science that is based on Newtonian mechanics.

Since the late nineteenth century, but especially in the last twenty years, a large group of natural scientists has been challenging the premises of Newtonian science. These scientists see the future as intrinsically indeterminate. They see equilibria as exceptional, and assert that material phenomena move constantly far from equilibria. They see entropy as leading to bifurcations that bring new (albeit unpredictable) orders out of chaos, and they therefore conclude that the consequence of entropy is not death but creation. They see self-organization as the fundamental process of all matter. And they express this view in some basic slogans: not temporal symmetry but the arrow of time; not certainty but uncertainty as the epistemological assumption; not simplicity as the ultimate product of science, but rather the explanation of complexity.[4]

Cultural studies attacked the same determinism and universalism under attack by the scientists of complexity. Cultural studies attacked universalism primarily on the grounds that the assertions about social reality that were made in its name were not in fact universal. Cultural studies represented an attack on the traditional mode of humanistic scholarship, which had asserted universal values in the realm of the good and the beautiful (the so-called canons), and analyzed texts internally as incarnating these universal appreciations. Cultural studies insisted that texts are social phenomena, created in a certain context and read or appreciated in a certain context.[5]

Classical physics had sought to eliminate certain "truths" on the grounds that these seeming anomalies merely reflected the fact that we were still ignorant of the underlying universal laws. Classical humanities had sought to eliminate certain appreciations of "the good and beautiful" on the grounds that these seeming divergences of appreciation merely reflected the fact that those who made them had not yet acquired good taste. In objecting to these traditional views in the natural sciences and the humanities, both movements—complexity studies and cultural studies—sought to "open" the field of knowledge to new possibilities that had been closed off by the nineteenth-century divorce between science and philosophy.

What the assault on Newtonian mechanics opened up in the collective psychology of social scientists was the possibility that their poor results in the public policy arena resulted not from the failings of the social scientists as empirical researchers but from the methods and theoretical assumptions they had taken over from Newtonian mechanics. In short, social scientists were now able to consider seriously for the first time the commonsense proposition they had so rigorously rejected: that the social world is intrinsically an uncertain arena.

What the assault on canonical appreciations of texts has opened up for social scientists is the obligation to be self-reflexive about the nature of their descriptions, propositions, and evidence, and to seek to reconcile the inescapability of positional bias in their work with the possibility of making plausible statements about social reality.

Thus, we enter the twenty-first century with considerable uncertainty about the validity of the disciplinary boundaries within social science, and a real questioning, for the first time in two centuries, about the legitimacy of the epistemological divide between the "two cultures," and hence the de facto threefold partitioning of knowledge into the supercategories of the natural sciences, the humanities, and the in-between social sciences. This uncertainty has arisen within a period of major transition for the university as an educational institution. It is this triple set of zones of decision, both intellectual and organizational, that I shall explore. I shall treat first the issue of the two cultures, then the issue of the possible restructuring of the social sciences, and finally the relation of these changes to the university system as such.

That the epistemological issues are basic to all the current debates is seen in the amount of passion the "science wars" and the "culture wars" have aroused in recent years. Passions usually run highest when participants in the arena believe, correctly or not, that major transformations are being proposed and may actually occur. But of course passions are not necessarily the most useful way to uncover or develop resolutions of the underlying issues.

There had long been one major problem in this "divorce" between philosophy and science. Before the eighteenth century, theology and philosophy had both traditionally asserted that they could know not one but *two* things: that which was true and that which was good. Empirical science did not feel it had the tools to discern what was good, only what was true. The scientists handled this difficulty with some panache. They simply said they would try only to ascertain what was true and would leave the search for the good in the hands of the philosophers (and the theologians). They did this knowingly and, to defend themselves, with some disdain. They asserted that it was more important to know what was true than to know what was good. Eventually some would even assert that it was impossible to know what was good, only what was true. This division between the true and the good is what constituted the underlying logic of the "two cultures." Philosophy (or more broadly, the humanities) was relegated to the search for the good (and the beautiful). Science insisted that it had the monopoly on the search for the true.

Most persons, however, were unwilling in practice to separate the search for the true and the good, however hard scholars worked to establish a strict segregation of the two activities. It ran against the psychological grain, especially when the object of study was social reality. In many ways the central debates within social science throughout its institutional history have been around this issue, whether there was some way of reconciling the search for the true and the search for the good. This desire to reunify the two searches returned, often clandestinely, in the work of both scientists and philosophers, sometimes even while they were busy denying its desirability, or even its possibility. But because the search was clandestine, it impaired our collective ability to appraise it, to criticize it, and to improve it.

We cannot of course know how far we will go in the next twenty-five to fifty years in the project of "overcoming the two cultures." Not everyone, by any means, is committed to the project. Far from it. There are many sturdy supporters of the continuing legitimacy of the epistemological divide, both within the natural sciences and within the humanities, and consequently within the social sciences as well. What we can say is that in the last thirty years of the twentieth century, the knowledge movements that have been opposed to the existing divide have, for the first time in two centuries, become serious movements with extensive support, a level of support that seems to be growing.

The major problem these two movements have at present, aside from the existence of stiff resistance to each within their own camp or faculty or superdiscipline, is that each movement has concentrated on pursuing the legitimacy of its critique against the prevailing, and previously little questioned, orthodoxy. Neither complexity studies nor cultural studies have spent much time trying to see whether and how they could come to terms with the other and work out with the other a genuinely new epistemology, one that is neither nomothetic nor idiographic, neither universalist nor particularist, neither determinist nor relativist.

The relative lack of contact between the two movements is not only an organizational problem; it also reflects an intellectual difference. Complexity studies still wishes to be scientific. Cultural studies still wishes to be humanistic. Neither has yet totally abandoned the distinction between science and philosophy. There is a long way to go before the two convergent intellectual trends might actually meet and establish a common language. On the other hand, the social pressure—both that coming from within the world community of pursuers of knowledge and that coming from social movements throughout the world—is strong, as very many scholars (not to speak of everyone else) are overwhelmed by a sense of confusion coming from the exhaustion of the geoculture that has prevailed for some two centuries.

It is here that social scientists may perhaps be called upon to play a special role. They are professionally concerned with and attuned to the problem of establishing normative frameworks, and they have been studying such processes throughout their institutional history. Furthermore, the convergent trajectories of the two knowledge movements have in fact been pushing both the natural sciences and the humanities onto the terrain of the social sciences, where social science expertise, such as it is, may be applicable.

It is far too early to see clearly the lines of any new epistemological consensus. Such a consensus would clearly have to address a series of long-standing issues, in ways that are more satisfactory than attempts hitherto:

1) Assuming that the universe is both real and eternally changing, how is it possible to perceive any more general reality than someone's irreproducible photographic snapshot of some momentary part of it? And yet, if one cannot do this to some reasonable degree, what is the point of any kind of scholarly activity?

2) How can we measure the impact of the perceiver on the perception, the measurer on the measurement? This is the Heisenberg uncertainty principle writ large. How can we get beyond both the false view that an observer can be neutral and the not very helpful observation that all observers bring their biases to their perceptions?

3) Given that all comparisons deal with similarities and differences, what plausible criteria can we establish for deciding on similarities and differences, given that simi-

larities are based on definitions that exclude and that differences are endless?

4) Given that we seem to be endlessly finding smaller entities and larger entities in the universe, and given the seamlessness of the universe as context for everything that occurs, what are the meaningful units of analysis that plausibly will aid our comprehension of the universe and all its parts?

As one can see, these are all philosophical questions, but they are all scientific questions as well. Can there possibly be two sets of answers to these questions, and two arenas of debate about them? We do not pretend that any of these questions will be resolved in the twenty-first century. But the structures of knowledge depend upon provisional consensuses about them. And it is not at all impossible that, as a result of the current attacks on the trimodal division of knowledge, a new provisional consensus might arise over the next twenty-five to fifty years. Furthermore, if it does, this will have profound implications for the organization of the university system (that is, the faculties), as well as, of course, the organization of scholarly research. And if this trimodal structure breaks down, then we have to ask where could what we now call the social sciences fit into any reorganized schema?

Whatever the weaknesses of the intellectual distinctions incarnated in the major social science disciplines as categories of knowledge, there is no doubt that they are organizationally quite strong. Indeed, they are quite possibly at the acme of their strength. Contemporary scholars, especially professors in universities and graduate students pursuing higher degrees, have a considerable personal investment in these organizational categories. They have, or are getting, degrees in specific disciplines. These disciplines control appointments to the university and curricula insofar as they are organized in departmental structures. There are major journals, nationally and internationally, associated with each discipline. (Indeed, the name of the discipline is usually part of the title of such journals.) In almost every country there are national associations of scholars in a particular discipline. And there is a series of international associations bearing the names of these disciplines.

Thus the disciplines as organizations largely control entry, award prestige, and govern career advancement in the scholarly hierarchy. They are able to enact and enforce "protectionist" legislation. They may doff their hats on public occasions to the virtues of "multidisciplinarity," but they are sure to emphasize at the same time the limits of the permissibility of the exercise.

In addition, the existing disciplines are "cultures," in the simple sense that they share biases and premises in the choice of research topics, the style of scholarly enquiry, and the required readings of the scholarly community. They have announced their respective cultural heroes (whom they have enshrined as "traditions"), and they repeatedly conduct the rituals necessary to revalidate the cultures. Few social scientists today fail to identify themselves, some more closely, some more loosely, with a particular discipline, and to assert, at least *sotto voce*, the superiority of their own discipline over its competing neighbors in the social sciences. One should not underestimate the extent and effectiveness of this cultural loyalty.

Nonetheless, two major forces are undermining this capacity of the existing disciplines to reproduce themselves. The first is the actual practice of the most active scholars. The second is the needs of the controllers of financial resources—university administrators, national governments, interstate agencies, public and private foundations.

Active scholars constantly seek to create small working communities of those who share interests. This practice has been enormously expanded, first by the growth of speedy air travel and now even more by the creation of the Internet. Small working communities are of two sizes. There are groups of actual collaborators on specific research projects, who may number fewer than a dozen. And there are the somewhat larger communities of those working on similar research projects, who may number in the hundreds. Unless, however, we define commonality loosely, they are seldom larger than this. If we now begin to look at the emergence of such "research communities" or "networks" in the past thirty years (a piece of global empirical research that, to my knowledge, has not been done), I think we will discover two things: the number of such networks has been growing overall; and the members of such networks are drawn without respect to disciplinary boundaries, with the result that almost none of them is drawn exclusively from a single category; indeed, many of them show a significant dispersion in disciplinary labels. We can all provide instances of such groupings, from brain studies and cognitive studies, to science studies and rational choice, to international political economy and world history. There are no doubt dozens, perhaps hundreds, more such groupings.

The key thing to observe about the intellectual stance of such groupings is that typically they find little use in the classical divides that provided the historical underpinnings of the intellectual separation of the disciplines: present/past; civilized/barbarian; and even market, state, and civil society. Those who participate in the multiple networks maintain their organizational affiliations because, for the moment, there is no advantage (and perhaps some risk) in renouncing them, but their scholarly work does not reproduce the categories.

Whenever, furthermore, they find the disciplinary categories an obstacle to their research projects, especially when it threatens their access to funds, they actively seek to persuade the controllers of financial resources to give priority to their "cutting-edge" conceptual formulations over "traditional" concerns of the social science disciplines. They do this by establishing "institutes" or other specialized structures— within the universities, in the form of operating foundations, or in extra-university autonomous structures of prestige (academies and institutes of advanced study). Note that here, too, as with the names of the disciplines, the historical trajectory has been curvilinear: from multiple names down to just a few and then to the growth again of multiple names; from multiple institutional structures to the concentration within the universities of scholarly activity, then the rise again of multiple structures.

It is at this point in the equation that the entry of the donors of financial resources affects the picture. The period since 1945 has seen a sea change in world education. Primary education has now become a universal norm and secondary education a requirement in all countries with a median or high GNP per capita. The same expansion has also occurred in tertiary education. As of 1945 university education had been reserved to a minuscule percentage of the age cohort. But it has expanded incredibly since then, reaching more than 50 percent in the wealthiest countries and growing significantly even in the poorest. As long as the world knew a period of economic expansion (essentially 1945 to 1970), this posed no problem. The necessary funds were easily available. But ever since, universities have been caught in the crunch of a constantly expanding student base (because of both population growth and growing social expectations about the amount of education that an individual should have) on one side, and tightening financial resources (imposed on them primarily by the states caught up in fiscal crises) on the other.

The consequences of this scissors movement have been multiple. One is what might be called the "secondarization" of university education, the constant demand of government and other administrative authorities that professors teach more frequently and teach larger classes. The second is the creeping flight of scholars, especially the most prestigious ones, to positions outside the university system, scholars who are likely thereby to find themselves in structures that ignore existing disciplinary boundaries.

The third, and possibly most significant, consequence is the problem university administrators (and ministries of education) face: reduced resources per capita at a time when the breakdown of strict disciplinary boundaries leads to ever increasing demands to create new special structures, departments, institutes—demands that are inevitably costly. This must lead these administrators to seek to resolve their financial problems via structural reform within the university, and therefore to reconsider the validity of existing structures.

Where, then, are we heading? To begin with, we must reconsider the role of the university as the virtually singular locus of the production and reproduction of knowledge. One might say that this role has been the result of a movement that began at the beginning of the nineteenth century and reached its culmination point in the period 1945 to 1970, but then began to decline and should decline even further in the twenty-first century. There will, of course, continue to be universities, but they will have increasingly to share space (and social funds) with other kinds of institutions.

Second, we are beginning to have a major epistemological debate, reopening the question of the "two cultures" and promising to be at once noisy, worldwide, and somewhat politicized. The question remains open as to what will come out of this debate. The answer depends in part on developments in the larger social world beyond the world of knowledge. It is by no means certain that the movement toward a new consensus that overcomes existing epistemological divides will succeed in developing a set of arguments that will impose themselves. It is possible that the movement will be frustrated, either endogenously because of the inability to resolve plausibly outstanding intellectual questions, or exogenously because of the strength of forces resisting it. In either case it would be very much in question whether we could tranquilly revert to the existing system. We could easily see a breakdown in any widespread acceptance of common scholarly norms. Indeed, this is what some claim is already happening.

If, however, a new consensus is achieved, it will necessarily call into question the existing trimodal division of the university into the natural sciences, the humanities, and the social sciences. If that disappears, what will replace it? A unified faculty of knowledge? Or a recentering of activities in the "professional" schools—medicine (as health services), law (as public policy), business administration (as institutional management), and so forth?

And if we have an epistemologically reunified faculty of knowledge, what kind of role will the existing social sciences play within it? In one sense, surely, a central role, since the reunification, as we have seen, involves the acceptance by both the natural sciences and the humanities of some of the long-standing premises of the social sciences, especially the social rootedness of all knowledge. But there is still the question of what kinds of departments would be constructed within such a whole. There is no way at this time to answer this question clearly. For while the principal nineteenth-century divides that were the basis of the multiple social science disciplines may have been undermined, there are other divides for which there continues to be much support, even though they too are being questioned today: macro-micro, the self (even the social self) and the societal (or group or collective identities). Nor have we yet seen the full impact that the concept of gender will have on how we formulate intellectual divisions within social science.

So much of the answers to these questions is tied to what happens in the world-system as social reality. Social science attempts to talk about what is going on. It constitutes an interpretation of social reality that at once reflects this social reality and affects it, that is at once a tool of the powerful and a tool of the oppressed. Social science is an arena of social struggle, but it is not the only one, and probably not the central one. Its form will be conditioned by the outcomes of future social struggles as its historic form was conditioned by previous social struggles.

What can be said about social science in the twenty-first century is that it will be an intellectually exciting arena, a socially important one, and undoubtedly a very contentious one. It is best that we go into this situation armed with a combination of some humility about what we currently know, some sense of the social values we hope to see prevail, and some balance in our judgments about the role that we can actually play.

3 The End of Certainties in the Social Sciences

How to live with uncertainty is probably one of the oldest social problems humankind has faced. Ten thousand years ago, when human beings knew less about the physical and social world than we do today, the uncertainties of life were probably quite frightening. They could not anticipate very well either short-term or long-term changes in their natural environment. They were unsure about whether they and their families would find even the necessary food and shelter to survive the immediate future. They were unsure how soon, and in what form, they would be facing deadly enemies, animal or human. They may even have blamed themselves for bringing about this unwanted uncertainty. This is what we probably imply in the myth of the "expulsion from the Garden of Eden."

Such uncertainty was doubtless very socially destabilizing, and the doubts themselves could only have reinforced the dangers. To reduce the dangers, therefore, humans appealed to sources of certainty: magic and magicians, the gods and their priests, collective and communal authority and those who incarnated and exercised this authority. This worked, up to a point. It reduced doubts and fears, and thereby helped to stabilize social structures. But of course all these sources of certainty were able to predict correctly, or even explain retroactively, only up to a point. There were endless surprises, and some of them were quite serious. Still, this was a self-referential model of analysis. When predictions turned out to be wrong, when unexpected and seriously disturbing events did occur, what was most often blamed was not the belief in the possibility of certainty or even the system of ascertaining certainty but the practitioners of the art of certainty—the magicians, the priests, even the emperors (who, in the Chinese phrase, were deemed to have lost the mandate of heaven).

The modern world-system, the capitalist world-economy required for its efficient operation a somewhat higher level of accuracy in forecasting, without which the investment process so central to its functioning would never have acquired the extensiveness and level of risk-taking that has enabled it to expand and flourish. There was consequently considerable social support and social sanction for a new mode of certifying truth, the mode we have come to call science or, more accurately, modern science.

The scientists had to create space for science within a world whose cultural values were still based on earlier modes of validating certainties. This creation of room for science was actually a two-stage process. First, the philosophers attacked the meaningfulness of revealed truths (those that could be known only, or at least best of all, to priests and clerical structures). The philosophers insisted that all humans had the innate capability to reason individually and thereby to perceive truth. To be sure, they acknowledged that this was not easy, and that some persons (namely, the philosophers) were able to do this much better than most other people. But the philosophers were primarily interested in denying the right of either religious authorities or political authorities to proclaim truth. One might say that this was the primary cultural message of what we now call

modernity, and that this message was more or less successfully translated into everyday belief over the past five centuries, and accepted by most people throughout the world.

Science, as a cultural activity, represented a further specification of the philosophers' claim to universal human
rationality as the source of truth statements. The scientists
raised the question, how do we know whether any given
person's claim to have discovered truth by reasoning is
valid, especially given that there are multiple and competing claims to discoveries of truth? The scientists answered
that truth claims had to be validated by empirical evidence,
which had to be collected in specific ways that could be
replicated by fellow members of the scientific subcommu-
nity. In effect, the scientists were insisting that it was not
any philosophers but only a subgroup of them, the scientists, who had the moral right to receive recognition as the
source of valid truth claims. In fact, by the nineteenth century the scientists had largely won out in this cultural war
and did indeed receive social acceptance as the only persons to whose this-worldly truth claims deference should
be paid.

This scientific credo had a curious feature. On the one
hand, the scientists proclaimed theoretically a total rejection
of authority as the basis of legitimating truth claims, and a
total egalitarianism about who might put forward legitimate
truth claims.

There was, they argued, a free marketplace of ideas. Any
and all persons might offer their truth claims in this market
and present whatever evidence they had to persuade others.
And then, somehow, the community would either accept
the truth claims as valid or reject them. There were no *a priori* limits, and the antiquity of a prior truth claim, now contested, was no argument in its favor.

But on the other hand, in practice, scientists did not mean it. They did not actually believe that all authority was illegitimate, or that any and all persons might put forward truth claims in the marketplace of ideas. They actually believed that the small subcommunities of specialists in every defined subfield of science constituted a collective authority that, although not infallible, should be deemed correct unless there was overwhelming evidence to refute them. And they actually believed that, with rare exceptions, only persons with certain specialized training were entitled to be taken seriously when and if they put forward truth claims in the marketplace of ideas. The scientists, when challenged, pointed to the fact that although in reality they were limiting entry, they were in principle (and every once in a while in practice) ready to make exceptions. Still, to a distant observer from another planet, the deference paid to scientists in the twentieth century might not have seemed all that different from the deference paid to magicians, priests, and communal authorities in times of yore.

This rule applied whether the truth claims they were making represented "certainties" or merely "probabilities." Whereas scientists promulgated obstinately the virtues of skepticism ("how do you know what you allege to know?"), and the limitations of current knowledge ("all truths are provisional"), they also insisted that certainty was intrinsically possible, and that therefore there could come a day when everything would be known about everything. This was the image of the deterministic world, so central to what we call modern science. God does not play dice with the universe, said Einstein, expressing the deepest commitment of modern science. Determinism was the centerpiece of Newtonian mechanics, itself in turn long considered to be the fundamental scientific program, the model for all other scientific efforts. Determinism was conjoined with linearity, equilibrium, and reversibility to add up to a set of minimal criteria for calling theoretical explanations "scientific."

We are all aware that in the past one hundred years, and particularly in the past thirty years, this Newtonian model of science has come under sustained and severe challenge within the belly of the beast, within physics and mathematics themselves. I shall not outline this challenge in detail. I shall simply point to the counter-slogans of this challenge: in place of certainties, probabilities; in place of determinism, deterministic chaos; in place of linearity, the tendency to move far from equilibrium and toward bifurcation; in place of integer dimensions, fractals; in place of reversibility, the arrow of time. And, I should add, in place of science as fundamentally different from humanistic thought, science as part of culture.

I wish to look at the impact on social science of this challenge to Newtonian science that comes from within science. And I wish to suggest what kind of social science we can build that is grounded in the realization that we have reached the cultural end of certainties. Social science was institutionalized in the late nineteenth century in the shadow of the cultural dominance of Newtonian science. I shall not review here the internal methodological struggles of the social sciences, as they sought to carve a space for themselves amid the two-culture split between science and the humanities. In the period after 1945, all the social sciences, but especially the nomothetic trio of economics, political science, and sociology, became increasingly quantitative and insisted very strongly on the presupposition of a deterministic social universe. The object of social science, they reiterated, was to discern universal covering laws akin to those they believed physics had been able to state. The main problem they encountered was that, in practice, they were unable to make even short-term predictions that turned out to be sufficiently correct to merit social applause. When pressed, social scientists attributed these failures to their collective immaturity as serious science. In short, they blamed their own level of competence and not their mode of theorizing.

What the assault on Newtonian mechanics has opened up in the collective psychology of social scientists is the possibility that the poor predictions resulted not from the failings of the social scientists as empirical researchers but from the methods and theoretical assumptions they took over from Newtonian mechanics. In short, social scientists are now able to consider seriously for the first time the commonsense proposition they had so rigorously rejected: that the social world is intrinsically an uncertain arena. I call this a commonsense proposition in that most persons, if asked, would see this assertion as so self-evident that they could not imagine that anyone (even social scientists) could think otherwise.

What I would like to explore is what happens to social science if we take this commonsense proposition, now argued as a scientific proposition by Prigogine and many others, as the basis of our work in social science. Let us start with the ancient image that the universe is like a flowing river, in eternal, endless flux. "You can't step into the same river twice." How can this image be reconciled with the idea that there are covering laws that govern the universe in every detail? It can only be reconciled if one assumes Laplace's demon, and presumes that a being outside the entire universe, knowing these laws, could have predicted every twist and turn in the river. What happens if we substitute for Laplace's demon the assumption that all processes tend to move away from their equilibria and that, when they move sufficiently far, they bifurcate—that is, that the system has arrived at a point such that there are two or more solutions to the equation describing the process? What happens in my view is that, while we continue to be required to search for regularities of processes within systems, the systems themselves are constantly moving far from equilibrium, and therefore at some point will be transformed, such that the regularities we have observed no longer hold even as an approximation of reality. That is to say, we have to live with a contradiction. On the one hand, all the "truths" we discern hold only within certain TimeSpace parameters, and therefore very little of much interest can be stated that is "universal." On the other hand, although all is ever-changing, the world is quite obviously not without some patterns of explanation for these changes, and the changes themselves fall into two different categories—those that are an intrinsic part of the regularities of the system, and those that involve the transition to or transformation into a different systemic context.

Prigogine tells us the following about bifurcations in natural phenomena:

> Bifurcations are a source of symmetry breaking. . . . Bifurcations are the manifestation of an intrinsic differentiation between parts of the system itself and the system and its environment. Once a dissipative structure is formed, the homogeneity of time . . . or space . . . , or both, is broken.
>
> In general, we have a succession of bifurcations. . . . The temporal description of any such systems involves both deterministic processes (between bifurcations) and probabilistic processes (in the choice of the branches). There is also a historical dimension involved. If we observe that the system is in state d_2, that means it has gone through the state of b_1 and c_1. (Prigogine 1997, 69–70)

Allow me to translate that view into the language we use in the social sciences. I shall call the systems with which we deal in the human social world "historical (social) systems," by which I mean some social whole that has spatial boundaries (even if they change over time) and that evolves historically over time. In order for us to call this social whole a system, we would have to argue that it was relatively self-sufficient and that, during its evolution, it maintained certain essential features intact. In order for us to speak of a system evolving, we would have to identify a moment at which it came into existence as a system. In order for us to speak of a systemic bifurcation, we would have to identify a moment (in the past, because we could never identify such a moment in the future for an existing system) when this system came into systemic crisis. In short, we would need to analyze three different time periods: the period of genesis; the period of the normal operation and evolution of the system; the period of bifurcation, or systemic crisis.

A close look at these defining characteristics of a historical system immediately makes apparent that each criterion involves measurements that are extremely difficult for us to make, at least at our present state of knowledge in the social sciences. How can one operationalize "relatively self-sufficient," given the fact that no system (perhaps not even the entire universe) is exempt from existing in a larger context that has at least occasional impact on its functioning (and perhaps much more than that)? How do we decide which features of a system can be considered essential and how do we measure that they are intact? How do we operationalize boundaries of a social system, especially given that we assume they are constantly changing? And how do we operationalize the moment of genesis of a system, or the moment of bifurcation/systemic crisis?

The answer has to be that none of these scientific tasks is the least bit easy, and all of them would give rise, in the case of any specific analysis of a historical social system, to enormous debate among social scientists. Still, the fact that there would be controversy over the validity and reliability of the data presented does not invalidate the theoretical model, nor does it mean that we can escape the responsibility of seeking to obtain such data. The fact that the data that could be obtained, or supplied by various sources, might give rise to quite different interpretations by persons differently placed in the historical social structure, does not mean that it is hopeless to arrive at relative and interim accord on the greater persuasiveness of some interpretations than others. It merely means that we must be self-conscious of the inevitable and unavoidable social biases of all the interpreters, and enter into our mental operations correctives that amend the results to reduce the effect of the multiple biases. In short, what we need is a methodological road map, itself filled with uncertainties, in order to ascertain plausible interpretations of uncertain social realities.

I think that one crucial element in this road map is a specification of how we use terms like change, crisis, and bifurcation. We can reduce the utility of such terms to nil if their definition becomes too vague. The great danger is that, since change is eternal, everything becomes defined as a crisis, every twist and turn in the road a critical bifurcation. Of course, in the sense that there is an irreversible historical process and that all past events are part of present reality and explain why the empirical realities of the present could not be other than what they are (since reality passed through a given pathway, following an infinite series of social choices, large and small), everything *is* a crisis and bifurcations do occur at every microsecond. But, at that point, we have said nothing more than "you can't step into the same river twice." Using such definitions vitiates all analysis, and reduces our scholarly task to that of rerunning the infinite history of the universe, a task that is both impossible and totally without point.

So, right away, we have to distinguish somehow between minor changes and major changes, between cyclical downturns and systemic crises, between choices and bifurcations. This is of course clearly implied in Prigogine's distinction between the deterministic processes that occur between bifurcations and the probabilistic processes in the choice of the branches. But when this concept is applied to social science, there seems to be a lot of slippage, and a lot of forgetting of the basic distinction. Let me therefore return to my sense that there are three moments of time in the analysis of any historical social system—that of genesis, that of ongoing operation, and that of systemic crisis. None of these three moments lasts a mere microsecond, although, clearly, when we speak of the ongoing operation of a system, we are normally referring to a much longer time span than the time span of either a genesis or a systemic crisis.

Most social science is in fact written about what is happening in historical systems during their ongoing operations. Of course, in some cases, this is in full consciousness of the fact that the onset and sunset of a historical system are special, different moments. But in many other cases (more than one would hope), the fact that historical systems have a finite temporal duration is lost from view, and scholars use data to compare situations in various instances that are located in quite different historical systems. Such comparisons can readily and easily lead to dubious, even quite erroneous or irrelevant, conclusions. It is here that the classic idiographic critiques of the generalizers can point to many instances of egregious scholarly misjudgment. However, if the analyses are kept within a single historical system, we can also with relative ease come up with sets of generalizations that seem plausible and replicable. And it is here that the defenders of a nomothetic mode find their greatest justification, allowing them to feel that their underlying epistemology has been validated.

I would like to offer a methodological guideline that would enable us to observe simultaneously the ways in which so-called essential features of the system remain intact and the ways in which the system is evolving in a direction far from equilibrium such that it will have to bifurcate at some point. I call this methodological guideline the search for cyclical rhythms and secular trends. The concept of cyclical rhythms assumes some kind of equilibrium, albeit usually a moving equilibrium. It also assumes that there is always "noise" in any process, such that there are always fluctuations, and that these fluctuations, when graphed, take the form of multiple cycles of varying lengths. Since there is always so-called noise, such cycles are inherent in all systems, whether physical or social, and they can be measured. Of course, there is no presumption that the pattern involves defined and unchanging time intervals. Quite the contrary: it is assumed that, in all complex systems, the most that can be described, because the most that really exists, are approximate standards, which show a high probability of recurrence. What needs to be demonstrated, however, is that there is something in the process that makes these fluctuations inevitable and recurrent, and that this something can be adequately delineated.

Of course, the number of rhythms that exist in a given historical system may be quite large, and one may wish not only to show that some are more important and/or longer than others, but also to explain the particular consequences of the more important rhythms. However, it may also be that, to explain other particularities, one would be better off noticing some of the allegedly less important rhythms. In any case, the description of the rhythms is the description of the operational features of the system. They are what allow us to call a system a system. Historical social systems are not special in this regard, only more complex, and it is therefore more difficult to measure, even approximately, these rhythms.

Since, in fact, the rhythms are always imperfectly symmetrical in reality because of the ever-changing detailed happenings of the system, the equilibrium is always moving, and it can usually be seen to be moving in a certain direction. This gives us what is often described in deterministic literature as the linearity of the system, and what we are calling secular trends. What is often left out of the analysis is that most trends, at least most trends in historical social systems, cannot be extended infinitely because they reach certain types of in-built limits. Let me illustrate with an obvious one. I suppose the population on the earth could expand indefinitely through biological reproduction. But at some point one would literally run out of space. And at some no doubt earlier point, one might run out of food supply. Something would thereupon happen that would reduce the size of the world population. So it is not in fact true that this linear vector could expand indefinitely. It would be very easy to make a long list of such indefinitely linear vectors that are in practice impossible to achieve.

What this immediately shows is that a vector cannot be analyzed as though it were in an autonomous trajectory, since its actual itinerary is the direct result of its interaction with other factors. Its development is dependent on certain specific conditions such that all systemic expansion has quantitative boundaries. I think, in fact, that it is not very useful to measure vectors as absolutes but always as relations with other vectors. In short, we should rethink what it is we should be measuring as secular trends. I believe that what we should be measuring are the percentages to be found in processes one has determined to be crucial to the operation of a particular historical social system. For example, in the modern world-system, I would be interested not in the number of full-time wage workers but in the percentage of the system's population that is engaged more than half-time in wage labor. I will not argue here why this is important. I merely wish to point out that, once one has converted data into percentages, there always exists the asymptote of 100 percent. Nothing can be true of more than 100 percent of the population being measured. It follows that all secular trends tend to reach a point where they cannot continue in a linear fashion. This, it seems to me, is precisely where historical systems reach crisis points, which therefore lead to bifurcations.

What then is the methodological relationship between cyclical rhythms and secular trends? It seems to me rather obvious. Why, after all, are cyclical rhythms in historical social systems cyclical? Evidently because when the operation deviates too far above or below the equilibrium, it becomes in the interests of some social players to act in ways that push the system back toward the equilibrium. In everyday language, adjustments are made. Of course, the nature of these adjustments is a function of the power structure of any system and the priorities built into the operating mechanisms of the system. And, of course, they do not occur smoothly because of the large number of actors and the large number of conflicting interests. But, generally speaking, we can predict what is likely to happen and therefore what has happened. This is basically what Braudel meant when he argued that "events are dust" and that, rather than recount the sequences of events, we must seek to discover what has been happening in the *longue durée.*

I think it would therefore be useful, at least in discussing historical social systems, to distinguish between minor and major uncertainties. Minor uncertainties are ubiquitous. No one ever knows what is really going to happen at the next instant. The virtually infinite number of potential actors plus the ever-changing physical environment render exact forecasting an intrinsic impossibility. But much of such uncertainty can be minimized. We can estimate probabilities with some degree of error, and I suppose one can argue that the "normal science" (in Kuhn's phrase) of the Newtonian paradigm as applied to the social sciences is precisely the attempt to make these estimates nearer and nearer to what eventually occurs. From the point of view of the larger social order, a decrease in an estimate's degree of error is without doubt a positive thing. Public policy is constantly being made on the basis of such estimates. Is it more important to invest social resources in expanding health facilities or improving earthquake-detection devices? The answer depends in part on our estimates of degrees of potential danger, and to whom the danger is most threatening.

I no more wish to deny the utility of such social scientific work than Prigogine is denying the utility, for many purposes, of classical Newtonian equations. But—and there is a but!—we must bear in mind three things about this "normal" Newtonian science. First of all, its legitimation is to be found in policy outcomes. In the natural sciences, we would say its legitimacy is to be found in technology or in engineering. Can you build better bridges as a result of this scientific work? Can you make more intelligent policy decisions as a result? Up to now the physicists and chemists have had a better score using this measuring rod than, say, the economists and sociologists. This is precisely what has impelled social scientists over the past century to try to "catch up" with the natural scientists. And, given both the external social pressure on them and the demands of their own superegos, it is quite understandable that social scientists have been attracted to the so-called nomothetic path. But given their really low score on social engineering, one might think that they would look again at whether this route pays off.

The second thing to say about following this path is that we have been blinded by the epistemological blinkers it has imposed upon us. It is the growing awareness of the negative effects of these epistemological blinkers that has fueled the knowledge movement within the physical sciences that bears the embracing label of "complexity studies." Once again, social scientists have been laggards, and they are only now beginning to look again seriously at the epistemological assumptions that underlie their chosen methods. They are beginning to return to "philosophy," a domain they had loudly ejected from their purview as "unscientific." This trend is not at all a negative thing, and I shall return to this question.

The third problem about doing "normal" Newtonian science, even in a probabilistic mode, is that it obliterates all knowledge about, and therefore concern with, the larger uncertainties in social reality. The larger uncertainties do not occur every day, or even every year or every decade. They may, in the case of historical social systems, occur only once every five hundred years. But it is these fundamental bifurcations that form the pattern of historical evolution of the human species and tell us what we really want to know: where we have been, where we are, and where we are likely to be going; or rather, which of our possible futures we might reasonably seek to realize because we prefer it.

Why do we avoid studying the fundamental bifurcations? In part, we are afraid to do so because their outcome is truly uncertain. In part, our attention is deliberately diverted from doing so in order that we not apply our collective efforts to affecting the outcome of the bifurcation in some ways, thereby permitting a minority (normally the privileged minority) to make their inputs into the process unimpeded. If, however, we decide consciously to look at systemic bifurcations, we require a quite clear picture of the considerable difference between everyday choices and systemic bifurcations. To put this into the language people use in daily life as well as in social science, we have to be aware that, historically, most so-called "revolutions"—whether political, economic, or other—have in fact been minor adjustments, and that the real upheaval of moving from one historical system to another may look very chaotic indeed and be very hard to classify.

At the present time the modern world-system finds itself in one of these fundamental bifurcations. It is in systemic crisis, and consequently there is also a crisis in our structures of knowledge. Hence we are confronted not with one but with two major social uncertainties. One is what will be the nature of the new historical system that we are constructing. The second is what will be the epistemology of the new structures of knowledge that we are constructing. Both involve struggles whose outcome is unpredictable, but each marks the end of the world as we know it. I am using "know" in its double sense: know, as to be acquainted with (*cognoscere, conocer, connaître, kennen*) and know, as to understand (*scīre, saber, savoir, wissen*). The modern world-system, the capitalist world-economy, is in crisis. We no longer know it. It presents to us unfamiliar landscapes and uncertain horizons. The modern structures of knowledge, the division of knowledge into two competing epistemological spheres of the sciences and the humanities, is in crisis. We can no longer use them as adequate ways in which to gain knowledge of the world. We are confused by our inability to know, in both senses, and many fall back on dogmatisms. We are living in the eye of the hurricane.

I shall not discuss the crisis in the capitalist world-economy. I have done it many times elsewhere (Wallerstein 1995a, 1998b). Suffice it to say that I believe there exists today, as a result of long secular trends that have been moving away from the equilibrium, a massive profit squeeze that will block the continuation of an endless accumulation of capital, the motor force of capitalist development. This squeeze results from at least three separate vectors: the secular rise of real wages across the world-economy as a whole; the growing destruction of the environment resulting from the institutionalized externalization of costs; and the fiscal crises of the states, which has been caused by the democratization of the world-system that has led to raising significantly the minimum levels of demand on the states for education, health care, and lifetime minimum-income guarantees. In addition, there has been a collapse in the legitimacy of the state structures because of growing disillusionment with the possibility of reducing the polarization of the world-system, and this legitimation had long been a key mechanism in maintaining the equilibrium of the world-system. I cannot argue this case now and must simply assert that there appears to be no solution within the framework of the existing system that would bring the system back to an even temporarily stable equilibrium. Therefore systemic parameters are oscillating wildly and a branching is occurring. We can assume that the elaboration of this bifurcation will occur over about half a century before a definitive choice is made, and a new system (or systems) come(s) into existence. We may further expect that this period will be one of great social turmoil, in part because of the fluctuations of the system, in part because of the decline of legitimacy of the state structures, and in part because there will be great conflict about the nature of the successor system.

Let me concentrate on the implications of this systemic bifurcation for the structures of knowledge. Structures of knowledge are of course an integral part of the cultural underpinnings on any historical social system. While there always exists a sort of internal logic of such structures, and therefore a somewhat autonomous intellectual trajectory, they are part of a larger structure, having to fit into the logic of this larger structure and constrained by the intellectual boundaries the larger system has put in place. Structures of knowledge are precisely that, structures, and as such they are brought into existence socially and can only survive socially if there continues to be long-term compatibility with the social environment.

Over the long period during which the modern world-system struggled to put in place a geoculture suitable for its optimal functioning, the epistemological unity of knowledge presumed in prior systems came under ever-increasing attack until, in roughly the last half of the eighteenth century, the so-called divorce between science and philosophy (or the humanities) was consummated. We can easily explain the social underpinnings and the historical process of this major reorganization of our conceptions of knowing. What is more relevant at the moment is the nature of the presumed division into "two cultures." Each camp argued that it had ways of knowing the world radically different from and significantly better than those of the other camp.

The scientists asserted that we could only know by empirical investigation (ideally, by experimentation) and that from such empirical investigations we could develop theorems that were testable in rigorous ways. As long as these theorems continued to pass successive tests (which in principle were unending), they could be said to state, at least provisionally, universal truths. If one were able to present an adequately replicated and validated hypothesis, one could make the claim that this truth was certain. It is not always clear what we mean by something being certain, but minimally it surely meant that we could count on getting the same mathematical results each time we used the equation, the variation being only in the data that were inserted, the so-called "initial conditions." Insofar as the state of knowledge about any given object of enquiry was insufficient to assert such universal truths, this was said to be the fault of the scientists themselves, who had not yet been able to arrive at this point of knowledge. But the epistemological expectation was that eventually the community of scientists would bring forward members who could demonstrate the universal truths pertinent to the object of enquiry. Certainty of analysis was a certain prospect.

The epistemological divide between science and philosophy has been directly challenged by two knowledge movements that have gained strength in the past twenty-five years. One is the sciences of complexity. It is a movement of many strands, and Prigogine is one major figure in its intellectual development. I have already indicated the main lines of its differences from Newtonian mechanics in its basic assumptions. I would just like at this point to underline its relationship to social science. I have already indicated the social-psychological impact of complexity studies on social science. It has undermined the cavalier argument of nomothetically oriented social scientists that they represented the incarnation of the scientific method. By doing this, the sciences of complexity have opened up space within social science for a different approach to science, one centering around the end of certainties. And this is very healthy and will be fruitful in itself.

There is, however, a second thing to say about the relation of the sciences of complexity and social science. One of the central slogans of the sciences of complexity is the "arrow of time," a phrase invented by Arthur Eddington and taken up and disseminated widely by Prigogine. For Prigogine, this is the response to a central theme of Newtonian mechanics, reversibility. In social science no one, not even the most hardy nomothetic advocates, has dared to argue reversibility. What the social scientists have done instead is ignore history, and indeed deplore "historicism."

By raising high the banner of the "arrow of time," by asserting in effect that even the tiniest units of physical matter have a historical trajectory, one that cannot be ignored, Prigogine not only has reinforced those social scientists who have always insisted that there can be no social analysis that is not historical, but also has moved physical science onto the central epistemological terrain of social science. He has renewed the call for a unified science, but not in the spirit of the analytic philosophers who wanted everyone to adopt the premises of Newtonian mechanics and become social physicists. Rather, he has in effect suggested that the natural scientists become part of a larger family in which the sociocultural premises and links of all knowledge activity be its unifying theme, one in which we overcome the two cultures because science and philosophy are conjoined activities deriving from a common epistemological base.

Meanwhile, at the other end of the spectrum, among the humanities there has emerged a vibrant and extremely diverse knowledge movement, now usually called cultural studies. Once again, I cannot develop here the historical origins of this movement or the reasons for its sudden explosion or the limitations of its analyses. I wish in this case, too, simply to indicate its relationship with social science. The importance of cultural studies is not that it has launched a critique of what its practitioners often refer to as Enlightenment views, but by which they centrally mean the cultural dominance of the premises of Newtonian mechanics. The sciences of complexity has made this critique better and more effectively. The real social contribution of cultural studies has been its critique of the humanities, as they had been institutionalized as a counter-dogma to science.

The humanities were not historically concerned with science; that, after all, was the point of the so-called divorce. They therefore looked askance at social science, which they saw as too committed to science, and encouraged its practitioners, particularly the historians, to define themselves as humanists and to locate themselves in faculties of philosophy. What they were concerned with were the criteria of evaluation of quality in the arts, broadly defined, as well as engaging in an empathetic, hermeneutic perception of social reality. This led them on the path to the establishment of canons, lists of aesthetic achievements that could be held aloft and taught to successive generations. In a curious way, they had reached the same point as the most committed Newtonian scientists. They were interested in perfection: elegance in art rather than elegance in theoretical formulation. But the point for both was that the worth of this excellence was not measured either by social utility or by criteria outside the internal rules of the knowledge activity.

Cultural studies arose in rebellion to this kind of aesthetic ivory tower. The practitioners of this new knowledge movement insisted that all cultural activity occurred within a social context, that it was produced and appreciated differently according to the social location of the producer or the appreciator. And, of course, the social location itself was a constantly evolving historical reality, such that how one appreciates a text today may be different from how the same person appreciates it tomorrow. Here, too, I wish to emphasize the relationship of these propositions to social science.

Social science has always been built around the assumption that we perceive social reality through socially constructed lenses. Even the most nomothetically oriented social scientists admit this, at least implicitly. They simply seek to overcome what they see as a limitation, whereas other social scientists take this so-called limitation as a permanent reality, one that actually promotes a richer understanding of the world. In any case, cultural studies, by laying emphasis on this central theme, has placed itself fully on the terrain of social science and has thereby aided in overcoming a false dichotomy between humanism and science.

So here we are today, on the verge of a major epistemological restructuring, a reunification of the methods of enquiry across the fields of knowledge, and one in which the terrain of social science will now be central, if not all-encompassing. Social science is after all the study of the most complex systems that exist, and therefore the most difficult to translate into systematic analysis. It is also the inevitable, if often unacknowledged, underpinning of what we have historically called humanistic studies. It is in fact the necessary activity of everyone, from physicists to literary scholars. Far from being a call for the imperialism of social science, this is a call for universal entry into social science.

We desperately need a collective intellectual discussion, and whether we call this discussion science, philosophy, or social science is a matter of great indifference to me. We live with the knowledge that uncertainty, at least long-term uncertainty, seems to be the only intractable reality. This means that self-reflective knowledge activities not only have to build this central reality into the practices they develop, if they are to expand our understanding of the world, but they must be ready to move from level to level of analysis in the search for more plausible explanations, which will allow for more informed choices. In the end, knowledge has to be about choices, and therefore about innovation, imagination, and possibilities. Choices involve responsibility, and scholars and scientists are precisely persons who, by opting for the activity, commit themselves to assuming the responsibilities of their assertions, their claims, their guesses, their suggestions of priorities. Isabelle Stengers, in her distinction between "requirements on" and "obligations of" the scientist, spells out the significance of assuming responsibilities: "The theme of 'rationality' changes in effect its signification according to whether it is placed under the heading of a requirement, in which case it is usually a vector of arrogance and infamy, or is placed under the heading of an obligation, in which case it is a synonym of risk and submission to a test, a test not for the public or for the incompetent but for the one who chooses to place his work within a practice that claims to be rational" (Stengers 1996, 90).

If reality is uncertain, there is no way to avoid choices. If we cannot avoid choices, there is no way to prevent the value commitments, preferences, and presuppositions of the analyst from entering the process of analysis. Even if we eliminate all such considerations at the conscious level, that is, if we insist on affecting a stance of moral neutrality before the object of our knowledge activity, these factors come back in at the unconscious level and at the level of what is permissible social discourse. And even if we bring these latter to the surface, we discover that there is an endless regression of contextuality, personal and collective biographies, that can never be eliminated because they constitute the psyche of the analyst. In short, there is no search for truth that does not involve arguments about the good and the beautiful.

Is, then, science, *scientia,* an impossible dream? I would argue the exact opposite. It is only when we accept the impossibility of the separation of knowing from wanting that we can begin to know better. What it requires is two things. First, we must be willing to expose premises, of ourselves and of others, in an analytic rather than an accusatory way. We can then debate the question, would we have different results of our research if the premises were altered? No questions about premises would be taboo.

And second, we need to have scientific communities composed of persons coming from every collective trajectory in order to discover what would be proposed when persons with truly different biographies examine the same data, explore the same problem. In social science this means the extensive and veritable internationalization of the social science community. We are still a long way away from this objective.

And finally, to return to my earlier point, we must learn to distinguish between minor and major bifurcations, between adjustments and systemic transformations, between explaining what is ongoing and what is exploding. This informs the issue of choices. For the choices one makes in adjusting an ongoing social system and those one makes in branching into two or more possible future social systems are not at all the same, and they cannot be made intelligently, either set of them, unless we are clear about the problems we are facing and examining.

I believe that we live in a very exciting era in the world of knowledge, precisely because we are living in a systemic crisis that is forcing us to reopen the basic epistemological questions and look to structural reorganizations of the world of knowledge. It is uncertain whether we shall rise adequately to the intellectual challenge, but it is there for us to address. We engage our responsibility as scientists/scholars in the way in which we address the multiple issues before us at this turning point in our structures of knowledge.

4 Braudel and Interscience
A Preacher to Empty Pews?

The Ecole des Hautes Etudes en Sciences Sociales groups the courses that it offers each year under categories, most of which are quite like those used by most other universities: anthropology, economics, and so forth. For a long time, however, they also had a category called "Interscience," and Fernand Braudel regularly gave his seminar under this rubric.

But what is interscience? To my knowledge, it is not a term that Braudel has explicated anywhere in his writings, except briefly in an interview he gave the year before his death (Braudel 1984b). But one can perhaps reconstruct what the term must have meant to him by looking at a series of texts he published in 1958–60, at a moment when he had just recently become president of what was then called the VIe Section of the Ecole Pratique des Hautes Etudes, to which he was giving very active intellectual leadership.

The first text is the very famous discussion of the *longue durée* in *Annales* (Braudel 1969a). Its opening sentence is: "There is a general crisis of the human sciences," and he ends the first paragraph with the suggestion that "one can envisage today [the] necessary convergence [of the human sciences]" (1969a, 81). Following his long discussion of multiple temporalities, which constitutes the heart of the article, he ends it with a peroration:

> On the practical level—for this article has a practical intention—I would hope that the social sciences stop for the moment arguing so much as to what their reciprocal boundaries are, what is or is not social science, what is or is not structure. Let them rather try to spell out, through their investigations, the elements (if elements there are) that could orient our collective research, the themes that would permit us to achieve a preliminary convergence. Myself, I believe these elements are: mathematization, narrowing in on (*réduction à*) locality, *longue durée*. But I would be curious to know what other specialists propose. . . . These pages are a call for debate. (Braudel 1969a, 83)

This is a striking paragraph in several ways. First, it is clear that what I would call the restructuring of the social sciences was very much on Braudel's mind in the midst of this, his most theoretical, text. He has, he says, a practical intention, and of course his entire career bears witness to how seriously he took this intention. Second, the text is a call for debate, a debate for which Braudel makes some preliminary suggestions. And third, his suggestion of elements for a convergence cuts across the epistemological divide that has informed the social sciences for a good 150 years. He calls for mathematization, dear to the hearts of quantitative, and usually positivist, social scientists. He calls for an emphasis on local specificity, dear to the hearts of those who are most critical of quantitative positivists. And he insists, of course, on the *longue durée*, which neither of those two quarreling groups tends to emphasize.

This paragraph is very open in spirit, but it does not deal per se with the knotty issue of resistance. Two years later Braudel published an article on "the unity and diversity of

the social sciences" in a journal dealing with higher education (Braudel 1969b). He starts out by noting that it is the
diversity and not the unity of the human sciences that
strikes the observer on first look. They seem to constitute
different "fatherlands" (*patries*), speaking different languages
and, to be sure, lodged in separate career channels. In this
article Braudel criticizes rather even-handedly all sides for
their narrowness of spirit, insisting that if there is to be convergence, the definition of who is to be included should be
very wide: "I maintain that, in constructing our unity, all
kinds of research are of interest to us, Greek epigraphy as
well as philosophy, or the biology of Henri Laugier, or public opinion polls, if they are carried out by someone imagi-
native and wide-ranging (*homme d'esprit*) like Lazarsfeld. We
too need an ecumenical council" (Braudel 1969b, 95).

Braudel concludes this article with the hope that the Maison des Sciences de l'Homme, over which he would come to
preside and which was not yet functioning at that time,
would incarnate the beginnings of this ecumenical council.

> All these young forces, all these new methods are within
> arm's reach, since we have assembled, perhaps uniquely in
> the world, the indispensable scholarly resources coming from
> all the "classical" human sciences, something that is extremely
> precious and without which nothing decisive is possible. Let us
> not fail to take advantage of this doubling or tripling of the
> odds. Let us hasten the movement that is tending, everywhere
> in the world, to move forward to unity. If necessary, let us skip
> stages, whenever this is possible and intellectually useful.
> Tomorrow, it will be too late. (1969b, 96)

Finally, let us look at his piece on history and sociology.
Braudel always gave a special place to discussing the relation
of these two classical disciplines, supposedly opposite in their
styles. His concern took the form of a lifelong discussion with

France's then-leading sociologist, Georges Gurvitch, and he wrote this piece for a textbook in sociology that Gurvitch was editing (Braudel 1969c).

In this piece Braudel's argument is quite radical. Unlike Gurvitch, as he explicitly notes, he categorically rejects the idea that history and sociology are different disciplines. He says that they constitute "a single adventure of the mind, not even just the obverse sides of a single cloth, but the entire cloth itself, in all the complexity of its threads" (1969c, 105). In this article, too, he ends with a peroration: "There can exist no social science, of the kind that interests me, without reconciliation, the simultaneous practice of our multiple métiers. Setting the social sciences one against the other is easy enough to do, but all these quarrels seem quite dated. We are in need of new music."

So there it is. Interscience is the totality of what has been paraded under the labels of the social sciences or the human sciences and indeed well beyond. It is the whole of them, not in the form of some confederation of principalities each of which is defending its domain against too much encroachment by the inclusive category, but as an interwoven cloth with countless threads. See how he put it in his 1984 interview:

> For me, there is only a unitary interscience. . . . If one tries to marry history and geography, or history and economics, one is wasting one's time. One must do everything, at the same time. . . . Interdisciplinarity is the legal marriage of two neighboring disciplines. I myself am in favor of generalized promiscuity. The devotees who do interscience by marrying one science with another are too prudent. It is bad morals that must prevail: let us mix together all the sciences, including the traditional ones, philosophy, philology, etc. which are not as dead as we claim. (Braudel 1984b, 22)

It is the final design, and nothing else, that is of interest to Braudel. In 1960 he called on us to rush forward to an ecumenical unity, for tomorrow will be too late. Is today tomorrow? Are we too late? It might seem so on first look. One sees precious few signs today of Braudel's passion to create a truly unified, singular social science in the very institutions that Braudel built and wherein he labored. Is the picture any better in the United States? I fear not. I take as testimony a piece published in September 1999 by an eminent American historian, president of the American Historical Association, and someone who knows France and the *Annales* well, since he is a distinguished historian of France as well, Robert Darnton. Darnton wrote a "letter" to all members of the AHA that he entitled "History Lessons" (1999, 2–3). Hear his voice:

> After a century of grand theory, from Marxism and Social Darwinism to structuralism and postmodernism, most historians have abandoned the belief in general laws. . . . Instead, we concentrate on the particular and sometimes even the microscopic (*microstoria*, as it is known in Italy)—not because we think we can see the universe in a grain of sand but because we have developed an increased sensitivity to the complexities that differentiate one society or one subculture from another. . . .
>
> Historians generally distrust the notion of parallels in the past or refuse to believe in their existence. . . .
>
> Twenty years ago, professional historians fell under the spell of the so-called *Annales* school—a group in Paris who attempted to write "total history" by studying shifts in the structure of society over long periods of time. That Olympian view no longer seems sustainable today. . . .

What then does Darnton offer us? He says that the world is "loaded with meaning, meaning shaped by past experience." This offers us "perspective." But, it seems, no one is listening. Most college students "increasingly neglect history to concentrate on economics, politics, computer science, and other varieties of systems analysis."

I will not take the time to analyze the fallacy in virtually every line of Darnton's text. I merely note that Darnton in this statement is virtually the anti-Braudel, as indeed he seems to intend. We have come full circle. Febvre and Bloch started *Annales* to combat the *histoire historisante* of Seignobos and the French historical establishment. And Darnton, in spectacular *vieux jeu,* brings us back to the starting point—and affects to feel besieged, at that.

So have we missed Braudel's golden opportunity—in France, in the United States, in the world? Perhaps yes, but then again perhaps not quite. Still, we should analyze why it is that the headlong rush toward a unidisciplinary historical social science, which Braudel was not merely promoting but believed was in process, has belied his optimism. There has been, first of all, perhaps foremost of all, the defensive posture of all those, in all the various loci of petty power in the realm of academia, who have resisted good ideas for bad reasons. Of course, Braudel himself was well aware of this phenomenon, having run into it personally throughout his career. Braudel was perhaps less inclined than we may think he should have been to analyze the forces outside academia who had every interest in maintaining the inability of the world's social scientists to explicate in analytical depth the realities of the world in which we live, and who therefore underpinned with their undoubted power the stance of the petty conservatives within academia.

Still, we should not content ourselves with arguing that Braudel's hopes and intentions for world social science were simply frustrated by its opponents. For the opponents have done less well than we may fear and than they may think.

Consider what has happened in the structures of knowledge since 1960. There was first of all the world revolution of 1968. Its principal consequence in the political arena is closely allied to its principal consequence in the world of academia.

In the political arena, it brought about the end of the world liberal consensus, which had culminated in the period after 1945 in a belief in the certainty of progress, the inevitability of socioeconomic convergence of the world's populations, and the central role of state reformism in achieving these ends. By breaking down this consensus, the world revolution permitted the reemergence of genuinely conservative forces and of genuinely radical forces. It thereby broke down the stultifying underlying conformism of the political and intellectual arena. It did this, however, without replacing the previous consensus with any clearly dominant integrating view. The world political arena has become one of great confusion and of large-scale popular rejection of the legitimacy of state structures. This has been one major element in a general structural crisis of our existing world-system. We have entered into an extended chaotic bifurcation with all its intrinsic uncertainties of outcome.

The impact of these stresses in the political economy of the world-system has been immediate and profound on the structures of knowledge. Braudel's vision of the interscience that was coming was essentially correct, but he didn't take into account the rocky perturbations of the crisis in the world-system, a crisis about which he would start to write after 1973 and which preoccupied him in the last decade of his life.

To appreciate what has been happening in the academic arena, we have to move back in time and understand how this arena had gotten to the point that Braudel was trying, in these early writings, to reorient it fundamentally. We need to start the story in the nineteenth century, with the creation of the modern university system, initially in western Europe and North America, and then by diffusion throughout the rest of the world. The modern university system is a structure of professional, salaried scholars, organized within subunits called departments that are united around what have been called disciplines. We need to remember that, as recently as 1850, hardly any of this existed anywhere.

Actually, the various departments that constitute the central core of the university, what in the United States we usually call the "arts and sciences," the disciplines that offer the Ph.D. as the culminating point of student training, have come to be organized by and large within superdomains usually called faculties. There are almost always at least two, and sometimes three, of these faculties. There exist virtually everywhere both a faculty of natural sciences and a faculty of the humanities (the names may vary slightly). In some universities there is in addition a third faculty, the faculty of the social or the human sciences. Braudel himself tried hard to establish such a faculty at the Sorbonne. And when he failed, he placed his hopes on the VIe Section and even more on the Maison des Sciences de l'Homme to play this role.

But why are there two (or three) faculties? Why not one? Before the nineteenth century, there was only one. It was called the faculty of philosophy (which is why, to this day, the highest degree, even in departments of physics, tends to be called the doctorate of philosophy). The idea that the single faculty should be divided in two (sciences and humanities) is the result of the so-called divorce between science and philosophy, and the reification of modern science as a separate method, a different theory of knowledge from philosophy, the only route (according to the scientists) to truth. Science, as it was now being defined, was more than merely another form of knowledge. It was the anti-philosophy, because philosophy was speculation and hence had no claims to be truth.

This modern development was the culmination of a long process that absorbed European thought during early modern times, the steady ghettoization of theology as irrelevant to knowledge of the natural world, and the restriction of the concept of causation from the four Aristotelian categories to that of efficient cause alone. This is not the place to recount this story, except to note that it was the underpinning of the structure of two faculties, which represented competing, indeed contradictory, epistemologies.

Science was universalist. Its argument was that there existed laws of the natural world that were true across time and space, and that the object of the investigator was to discern and demonstrate these laws. The process was a cumulative one. These laws were said to be linear, deterministic, and time-reversible. The best law was the most general and the most economical in statement. The humanities, by contrast, were particularistic. Their argument was that they were concerned with moral and aesthetic values. While there was some claim that these values were general (as, for example, the Kantian categorical imperative), their actual expression took an infinite number of forms, and the object of scholars was to understand, hermeneutically, these various forms. One could not infer from one situation to another, since each situation was the result of its own particular history.

For the past two centuries we have built our academic structures on the assumption that never the twain (science and philosophy) shall meet. They were the "two cultures." The social (or human) sciences were caught in between. The various disciplines tended to choose sides in the great epistemological debate. The so-called nomothetic disciplines (particularly economics, political science, and sociology) tended to be scientific, or at least scientistic. Anthropology, Oriental studies, and history affected more humanistic, or hermeneutic epistemologies. They emphasized variety, not similarities, in human social behavior.

What Braudel was trying to do—and of course he was not alone—was to overcome the gulf within the social sciences, to assert that both epistemologies were mistaken, to call for a reunification or, as he said, an ecumenical congress. If he seems today not to have succeeded, it is because he succeeded too well, attracted too much support, and there came to be a backlash—in France, in the United States, and elsewhere—against what were perceived as his heresies. But his harshest opponents can do little better than reassert the old tunes against the call for new music. Darnton's "letter" is nothing but a reassertion of all the old "humanistic" themes.

Meanwhile, two important intellectual developments have occurred, neither of which was yet visible in 1958–60. On the one hand, within the natural sciences and mathematics themselves, there has arisen a new intellectual movement, these days usually called the sciences of complexity. These natural scientists are challenging the classical Baconian-Cartesian-Newtonian epistemology, codified in the nineteenth century by Laplace. They are rejecting determinism, linearity, time-reversibility, and the eternal return to equilibria. They are arguing that not merely humans but atoms and galaxies are to be analyzed as the result of the "arrow of time." They are saying that the universe is intrinsically uncertain, and therefore that all matter operates creatively. Ilya Prigogine has extended Braudel's calls for ecumenicism. He not only wants to reconcile history and sociology; he wants to reconcile history and physics. See, for example, the 1994 conference of which he was the key figure, sponsored by the departments of history and of physics of the University of Pavia, and entitled "Con Darwin al di là di Cartesio: la concezione 'storica' della natura e il superamento delle 'due culture'" ("With Darwin and Beyond Descartes: The 'Historical' Conception of Nature and Overcoming the 'Two Cultures'"). Nor is this the old idea of the Vienna Circle that knowledge should be reunified via everyone's acceptance of the primacy and sole legitimacy of Newtonian science. Rather, it is the open hand of equal to equal. If anything, it is being argued that the natural sciences need to relearn their paths by incorporating the accumulated wisdom of the historians.

And in the humanities there has arisen in the past three decades that very strong and controversial movement we call cultural studies. Cultural studies is a much misunderstood movement—in part because so many of its practitioners themselves misunderstand what it is they are doing. The fundamental intention of cultural studies is not a sort of nihilistic destruction of knowledge, the total solipsistic relativism peddled by a few extremists. Rather, their historical mission has been twofold. On the one hand, they have demonstrated that the so-called canons of good taste put forward by so many within the humanities are socially constructed and therefore truly particularistic. And on the other hand, the fact that particularistic canons have been put forward as universal norms is a product of the unequal hierarchies of the modern world-system, and has served to sustain those in power in this system.

Note what has been happening. At the time that Braudel was writing these texts, the social sciences were still fighting for their legitimate place in the university (remember his failure to create such a faculty at the Sorbonne), and were being torn apart by the contending claims of the two superdomains, each saying "choose us, or you are worthless." It is in this ambiance that Braudel preached reunification of the social sciences. It was a call for intelligent reflection; it was a call, too, to self-confidence. The social sciences did not need to prove themselves by false standards, whether they were called scientific or humanistic standards.

Today, however, as a result of the emergence of these two vigorous movements of the sciences of complexity and of cultural studies, those "young forces" that Braudel celebrated, which are located in these two arenas, are moving centripetally toward the middle arena, that of the social sciences, rather than pulling away from each other centrifugally, as was for so long the case. To be sure, the "young forces" are not unopposed. The nostalgics of another era, the defenders of a sterilized status quo, those fearful of the possibilities of creative change, are shouting *haro!* They are launching science wars and culture wars, and seeking to intimidate us all back into silence.

They are trying to ignore Braudel's call for a radical conception of interscience—in France, in the United States, and elsewhere. Since we are living in an age of transition, where outcomes are uncertain, I will not say that they cannot succeed. But they need not succeed. It depends on us. And the battle within the academic arena is part and parcel of the larger battle within the world-system about the kind of successor world-system we wish to create. We shall only be able to contribute to these battles if we see them lucidly and not allow the "dust" of irrelevant *vieux jeux* to cloud our vision. We should return to Braudel's three elements that would permit a preliminary convergence of the human sciences: mathematization, narrowing in on locality, and *longue durée*. From there we may move forward to a more sophisticated restatement of the common epistemology that should inform all exercises in knowledge. It will take time and effort.

5 Time and Duration

The Unexcluded Middle,
or Reflections on
Braudel and Prigogine

While epistemological debates are no doubt eternal, there are moments when they seem to reach higher intensity than usual. We have been living such a moment since the last decades of the twentieth century. Science appears to be, is said to be, under fierce attack, and with it rationality, modernity, and technology. Some see this as a crisis of civilization, of Western civilization—even the end of the very concept of a civilized world. Whenever the defenders of prevailing intellectual concepts seem to be screeching in pain rather than ignoring their critics or answering them calmly and (dare I suggest) rationally, it may be time to take a step backward in order to make a cooler appraisal of the underlying debate.

For at least two centuries now, science has been enthroned as the most legitimate path, even the only legitimate path, to truth. Within the structures of knowledge this has been sanctified by the belief that there exist "two cultures"— that of science and that of philosophy (or letters)—which have not only been thought to be incompatible with each other but have also been de facto ranked in a hierarchy. As a result, the universities of the world have almost everywhere separated these two cultures into distinct faculties. If the universities have asserted formally the view that the two faculties were equally important, governments and economic enterprises have not hesitated to manifest a clear preference. They have invested heavily in science and for the most part barely tolerated the humanities.

The belief that science is something different from and even antagonistic to philosophy, the so-called divorce between the two, is in fact relatively new. It evolved as the endpoint of the process of the secularization of knowledge that we associate with the modern world-system. Just as philosophy came to displace theology as the basis of statements of truth by the end of the Middle Ages, so science came to displace philosophy by the end of the eighteenth century. I say "science" did this, but it was a very particular version of science, that associated with Newton, with Francis Bacon, and with Descartes. Newtonian mechanics posited a series of premises and propositions that achieved canonical status in our modern world: systems are linear; they are determined; they tend to return to equilibria. Knowledge is universal and can ultimately be expressed in simple covering laws. And physical processes are reversible. This last statement is the one that seems most counterintuitive, because it suggests that fundamental relations never change and that time is therefore irrelevant. Yet this last proposition is essential if one is to maintain the validity of the other parts of the Newtonian model.

Thus, in terms of this model, "time and duration" cannot be a meaningful or significant topic, or at least not one about which scientists can make statements. How can this be? To understand this, we have to take into account the history of the epistemological debates in the nineteenth and twentieth centuries.

Let me start with social science. Social science is a concept that was invented quite recently, only in the nineteenth century. It refers to a body of systematic knowledge about human social relations that was put forward and institutionalized in these two centuries. In the division of knowledge into two cultures, social science inserted itself as somewhere and somehow in between. It is crucial to note that most social scientists did not do this boldly, asserting the legitimacy (not to speak of the superiority) of some third culture. Social scientists intruded in between uneasily, uncomfortably, and with divided ranks. Social scientists continually debated whether social science was closer to the natural sciences or to the humanities.

Those who considered social science nomothetic, that is, in search of universal laws, generally argued that there was no intrinsic methodological difference between the scientific study of human phenomena and the scientific study of physical phenomena. All seeming differences were extrinsic, and were therefore transitory, if difficult to overcome. In this view, sociologists were simply backward Newtonian physicists, destined in principle one day to catch up. The road to catching up involved the replication of the theoretical premises and the practical techniques of the elder-brother disciplines. From this point of view, time (that is, history) was as little relevant to nomothetic social scientists as it was to solid-state physicists or microbiologists. What was far more relevant was the replicability of the data and the axiomatic quality of the theorizing.

At the other end of the spectrum of the social sciences stood idiographic historians, who insisted that human social action was nonrepetitive, and therefore not susceptible to large-scale generalizations that held true across time and space. They emphasized the centrality of diachronic sequences—history as stories, as narratives—as well as the aesthetics of literary style. I suppose it could not be said that they rejected time altogether since they emphasized, indeed embraced, diachrony, but their time was exclusively chronological time. What they ignored was duration, because duration could only be defined by abstraction, by generalization, and indeed by a chronosophy. Usually these scholars preferred to call themselves humanists, and they insisted on being located in the faculty of letters to indicate their disdain for nomothetic social science.

But even these humanistic, idiographic historians were caught up in the idolatry of Newtonian science. What they feared far more than generalizations (and therefore science) was speculation (and therefore philosophy). They were Newtonians *malgré soi*. They conceived of social phenomena as atomic in nature. Their atoms were historical "facts." These facts had been recorded in written documents, largely located in archives. They were empiricists with a vengeance. They held to a very up-close vision of the data and the faithful reproduction of the data in historical writing. Up-close tended to mean very small-scale in both time and space. So these humanist historians were also positivist historians, and most of them saw little contradiction between the two emphases.

This definition of the tasks of the historian became ascendant throughout the academic world between 1850 and 1950. It was not, to be sure, without its harsh critics. One major such current was in France and the journal *Annales,* founded by Lucien Febvre and Marc Bloch. In a letter written in 1933 to Henri Pirenne, who shared their discomfort with positivist history and whose influence on the *Annales* school was profound (see Lyon and Lyon 1991), Lucien Febvre described a book by Henri Seignobos as characterized by "a dusty, old-fashioned atomism, a naive respect for 'facts,' for the tiny fact, for the collection of tiny facts which are thought to exist 'in themselves'" (154). But the clearest and fullest statement of the critique of the dominant mode of historical writing was that made in 1958 by Fernand Braudel, who continued the *Annales* tradition after 1945 (Braudel 1969). I shall examine that text.

Let us start with the title, "History and Social Science: The *longue durée.*" If there is one term that is thought to summarize Braudel's emphasis and contribution, it is the *longue durée.* This is of course the duration of which we are speaking, although in fact Braudel's term tends not to be translated when used in English-language social science. The term is polemical. Braudel wishes to attack the predominant practice of historians to concentrate their energy on recording short-term happenings or events, which he calls (following Paul Lacombe and François Simiand) *l'histoire événementielle.* (This latter is a term difficult to translate into English; I believe the closest equivalent is "episodic history.")

For Braudel, the mass of "small details" (some dazzling, some obscure) that make up the bulk of traditional history (which is almost always political history) is only a part of reality, indeed only a small part. Braudel notes that nomothetic social science "is virtually horrified by events. Nor is this without reason: short time is the most capricious, the most deceptive duration" (Braudel 1969, 46). This assessment is the clue to Braudel's famous *boutade* in *La Méditerranée:* "Events are dust" (1966, II, 223).

Thus, against the chronological time of events, Braudel counterposes duration, *la longue durée,* with which he associates the term of "structure," giving the latter a very precise definition: "By *structure,* social analysts understand something organized, something coherent, relatively fixed relations between social realities and groups. For us historians, a structure is no doubt something put together, an architecture, but even more a reality that time affects only slightly and maintains over a long period. . . . All structures are simultaneously underpinnings and obstacles" (1969a, 50).

Against a time that is just there, a mere external physical parameter, Braudel insists on the plurality of *social* times, times that are created and, once created, both aid us in organizing social reality and exist as constraints to social action. But having asserted the limits and misdeeds of *l'histoire événementielle*, he is quick to add that it is not only the historians who are at fault: "Let us be fair. If there are those who sin by leaning to centering analysis around events, history, albeit the main culprit, is not the only guilty party. All the social sciences participate in this error" (1969a, 57).

It seems, says Braudel, that nomothetic social science is no more virtuous than idiographic history in this regard. He focuses his discussion on Lévi-Strauss's search for underlying social relations that exist in all social interaction, a set of elementary cells that are both simple and mysterious (once more, our atoms), which the scientist is supposed to seek to "perceive no matter what the language, translating them into Morse code" (1969a, 71). To this, he says no, this is not what I mean by *longue durée*. Quite the contrary:

> Let us reintroduce duration into what we do. I've said that models were of varying duration. The time of which they speak is valid insofar as it represents a particular reality. . . . I have compared models to ships. Shipwrecks are perhaps the most significant moment. . . .
>
> Am I wrong to think that the models of qualitative mathematics . . . do not lend themselves well to such voyages, above all because they circulate on only one of the numerous routes of time, that of the long, the *very long,* duration, sheltered from all accidents, cyclical movements, ruptures? (1969a, 71–72)

Thus, says Braudel, the search for the infinitely small (by the idiographic historian) and the search for not long but *very* long duration (by the nomothetic social scientist)—he says of the very long, "if it exists, [it] cannot be anything but the time of sages" (1969a, 76)—share the same defect. Braudel ends by making two claims, in effect. First, there are multiple social times that interweave and owe their importance to a sort of dialectic of durations. Hence, second, neither the ephemeral and microscopic event nor the dubious concept of infinite eternal reality can be a useful focus for intelligent analysis. We must rather stand on the ground of what I shall call the unexcluded middle—both time and duration, a particular and a universal that are simultaneously both and neither—if we are to arrive at a meaningful understanding of reality.

Braudel saw traditional history as privileging time (a certain time) over duration, and he sought to reinstate *la longue durée* as a key epistemological tool for social science. Prigogine sees traditional physics as privileging duration (a certain duration) over time, and he seeks to reinstate the arrow of time as a key epistemological tool for the natural sciences.

Here, too, a history of the controversy seems necessary for understanding the debate. The history of the natural sciences in the past two centuries is somewhat different from that of the social sciences. Newtonian science has followed a steady trajectory since at least the seventeenth century, both as an intellectual construct and as an ideology for the organization of scientific activity. By the early nineteenth century, it was given canonical (and, if you will, textbook) status by Laplace. Many of its practitioners felt that major scientific theorizing was at an end, and that all that was left for working scientists was to clean up some of the minor loose ends, as well as to continue to use the theoretical knowledge for practical purposes.

But, as we know, or as we should know, theorizing (just like history) is never at an end, because all our knowledge, however valid it seems in the present, is in a cosmic sense transitory because it is tied to the social conditions out of which it was learned and constructed. In any case, Newtonian science came up against physical realities it found difficult to explain, and by the end of the nineteenth century, when Poincaré demonstrated the impossibility of solving the three-body problem, it was in trouble, even though most scientists were not yet ready to acknowledge this.

Only in the 1970s did the discomfort with Newtonian mechanics as the paradigm for all scientific activity become sufficiently widespread that we can speak of a significant intellectual movement within the natural sciences challenging the predominant (and until then substantially unchallenged) views. This movement goes by many names. For shorthand purposes, it may be called "complexity studies." One of the central figures of this challenge has been Ilya Prigogine, who received the Nobel Prize for his work on dissipative structures. I shall use as my text his recent summation of his views, *The End of Certainty,* which has as its subtitle *Time, Chaos, and the Laws of Nature* (1997). Just as we may take the *longue durée* to signal Braudel's central emphasis, so we may take the "arrow of time" (a term Prigogine took from Arthur Eddington but that is now associated with him) to signal Prigogine's central emphasis.

As his point of departure in this book, Prigogine reproduces the conclusions he (and Isabelle Stengers) drew in their earlier *La nouvelle alliance*:

1. Irreversible processes (associated with the arrow of time) are just as real as the reversible processes described by the fundamental laws of physics; they do not correspond to approximations added to the basic laws.
2. Irreversible processes play a fundamental constructive role in nature. (Prigogine 1997, 27)

Newtonian mechanics, says Prigogine, describes stable dynamic systems. But just as, for Braudel, *l'histoire événementielle* described a part, but only a small part, of historical reality, so for Prigogine, stable dynamic systems are a part, but only a small part, of physical reality. In unstable systems, slightly varying initial conditions, which are always and necessarily particular, produce vastly different results. The impact of initial conditions is essentially unexamined within Newtonian mechanics.

And just as, for Braudel, the effects of the *longue durée* are most clear in macroscopic as opposed to microscopic structures, so for Prigogine, "it is indeed in macroscopic physics that irreversibility and probability are the most conspicuous" (1997, 45). Finally, just as for Braudel, "events are dust," so for Prigogine, "for *transient* interactions . . . diffusive terms are negligible" (1997, 44). The situation, however, becomes quite the opposite for Prigogine in Braudel's *longue durée*: "In short, it is in *persistent* interactions that the diffusive elements become dominant" (1997, 54).

For Braudel, there are multiple social times. It is only of the *very* long duration (a duration of which, I remind you, he said, "if it exists, it can only be the time of the sages") that truly universal laws may be asserted. Such nomothetic social science presumes the ubiquity of equilibria, as does Newtonian mechanics. Here, too, Prigogine takes aim: "Near equilibrium laws of nature are *universal*, but when they are far from equilibrium they become mechanism dependent. . . . Matter acquires new properties when they are far from equilibrium. . . . Matter becomes more 'active'" (1997, 65). Nor is Prigogine embarrassed by the concept of an active nature. Again, quite the contrary: "It is because we are at the same time 'actors and spectators,' to use Bohr's words, that we can learn something about nature" (1997, 150).

There is, however, one important difference between Braudel and Prigogine, their starting point. Braudel had to fight against a dominant view in history that ignored structure, that is, duration. Prigogine had to fight against a dominant view in physics that ignored non-equilibria situations and the consequences of the uniqueness of initial conditions, that is, time. Hence Braudel talked of the importance of the *longue durée* and Prigogine of the importance of the arrow of time. But just as Braudel did not want to leap out of the frying pan of *l'histoire événementielle* into the fire of the *très longue durée*, but insisted on staying in the unexcluded middle, so Prigogine does not seek to renounce reversible time to jump into the fire of the impossibility of order and explanation.

Prigogine's unexcluded middle is called deterministic chaos: "Indeed, the equations of motion remain deterministic, as is the case in Newtonian dynamics, even if a particular outcome appears to be random" (1997, 31). Well, perhaps more than just "appears to be," because he also says that "probabilities . . . acquire an intrinsical dynamical meaning" (1997, 35). This is why I speak of this position as being situated in the unexcluded middle. It is clearly middle: "What we have tried to follow is a narrow path between two conceptions that both lead to alienation: a world ruled by deterministic laws, which leaves no place for novelty, and a world ruled by a dice-playing God, where everything is absurd, acausal, and incomprehensible" (1997, 187–88).

Prigogine himself calls this "an 'intermediate' description" (1997, 189), but I wish to insist that it is not merely the assertion of the merits of a golden mean but those of the unexcluded middle—a determinist chaos and a chaotic determinism; one in which both time and duration are central, and constantly constructed and reconstructed. This may not be a simpler universe than the one classical science thought it was describing, but the claim is that it is closer to being a real universe, harder to know than the one we used to perceive, but more worth knowing, more relevant to our social and physical realities, ultimately more morally hopeful.

Let me conclude with two quotations. The first is from the great Belgian scholar, Henri Pirenne. He wrote this article, "La tâche de l'historien" ("The task of the historian"), in fact, specifically for an American casebook on methods in social science:

> All historical constructs . . . are based on a postulate: that of
> the identity of human nature over the ages. . . .
>   [Still,] . . . it takes but a moment of reflection to understand
> that two historians, looking at the same material, will not treat
> it in the identical way. . . . Thus, historical syntheses depend
> to a very great degree, not only on the personality of their
> authors, but also on their religious or national social surround-
> ings. (Pirenne 1931, 16, 19–20)

The second is from the American philosopher Alfred North Whitehead:

> Modern science has imposed on humanity the necessity for
> wandering. Its progressive thought and its progressive tech-
> nology make the transition through time, from generation to
> generation, a true migration into uncharted seas of adventure.

The very benefit of wandering is that it is dangerous and needs skill to avert evils. We must expect, therefore, that the future will disclose dangers. It is the business of the future to be dangerous; and it is among the merits of science that it equips the future for its duties. (Whitehead 1948, 125)

I opened by saying that science is said to be under severe attack today. It is not true. What is under severe attack is Newtonian science. What is under severe attack is the concept of the two cultures, of the incompatibility of science and the humanities. What is being constructed is a renewed vision of *scientia*, which is a renewed vision of *philosophia*, whose centerpiece, epistemologically, is not merely the possibility but the requirement of standing in the unexcluded middle.

6 The Itinerary of World-Systems Analysis, or How to Resist Becoming a Theory

The term "theory" tends to evoke for most people the concept of a set of interconnected ideas that are coherent, rigorous, and clear, and from which one may derive explanations of empirical reality. The term also denotes, however, the end of a process of generalization and therefore of closure, even if only provisional. In the construction of adequate or plausible explanations of complex phenomena, proclaiming that one has arrived at a theory often imposes premature closure on scientific activity, and therefore can be counterproductive. The more complex the reality, the more this tends to be true. I believe it is often better in such cases to explore empirical reality using spectacles that are informed by theoretical hunches but not bound by them. It is because I believe that this is eminently the case in the explanation of historical systems, which are large-scale and long-term, that I have long resisted the appellation of world-systems *theory* for the kind of work I do, insisting that I was engaged instead in world-systems *analysis*. This is thus the story of the itinerary and growth of a non-theory, which I call world-systems analysis.

83

The story begins for me in the 1950s, when I entered the graduate program in sociology at Columbia University. My principal empirical interest was contemporary politics, in the United States and the world. Columbia sociology at the time was considered to be the center of structural-functional analysis, and the department was particularly proud of pursuing research that combined the theorizing of Robert K. Merton with the methodological approaches of Paul F. Lazarsfeld. What is less often noticed is that Columbia was also the center of a major new subfield of sociology, political sociology (Wallerstein 1995c). At the time, its faculty (and visitors) included S. Martin Lipset, Daniel Bell, and Johan Galtung, all of whom were prominently associated with political sociology, plus Robert S. Lynd, C. Wright Mills, Herbert Hyman, Ralf Dahrendorf, Daniel Lerner, as well as Lazarsfeld, all of whom in fact did political sociology under other rubrics.

Political sociology was a thriving and growing field. One of the very first research committees of the newly founded International Sociological Association took political sociology as its subject. The Social Science Research Council sponsored a multiyear, multivolume project through its Committee on Comparative Politics. It was obvious to me that I would consider myself a political sociologist.[1]

I did have one peculiarity, however. I did not believe that the Cold War between the Western "free world" and the Soviet "communist world" was the primary political struggle of the post-1945 arena. I considered the main conflict that between the industrialized nations and what came to be called the Third World,[2] also known as the struggle of core vs. periphery, or later still of North vs. South. Because of this belief, I decided to make the study of contemporary social change in Africa my main scholarly pursuit.[3] The 1950s was a period in which the Western world took its first serious look at what was happening outside its own redoubt. In 1955 the Bandoeng conference of Asian and African independent states was the moment of self-assertion by the non-Western world, the moment at which it laid claim to full participation in world politics. And 1960 was the Year of Africa, the year in which sixteen African states became independent; it was the year also of the Congo crisis, which led to massive United Nations involvement in its civil war, a civil war that was bedeviled by much outside interference.

The year 1960 was also the year in which I came to know Frantz Fanon, an author I had long been reading and a man whose theorizing had a substantial influence on my own work. Fanon was a Martinican and a psychiatrist who went in the latter capacity to Algeria, where he became a militant of the Algerian Front de Libération Nationale. His first book, *Black Skin, White Masks* (first published in French in 1952), is about the psychic impact on Blacks of White dominance. The book was revived and widely republished in the 1990s and is still considered highly relevant to the discussions on identity that have become so prevalent. At the time, however, it was his fourth and final book, *The Wretched of the Earth* (published in French in 1961, just before Fanon's premature death from leukemia, with a preface by Jean-Paul Sartre), that made him world-famous. The book became in a sense the manifesto of the world's national liberation movements, as well as of the Black Power movement in the United States.

In the best tradition of both Freud and Marx, Fanon sought to demonstrate that what on the surface was seemingly irrational, notably the use of violence by these movements, was beneath the surface highly rational. The book was therefore not merely a polemic and a call to action but a reflective work of social science, insisting on a careful analysis of the social basis of rationality. I wrote a number of articles at the time, seeking to explain and defend Fanon's work (Wallerstein 1968, 1970, 1979), and I returned to the issue in my discussion of Freud and rationality in my presidential address to the International Sociological Association in 1998 (Wallerstein 1999).

The 1960s was a period of cascading independence in Africa. It was also a period of the first postindependence difficulties—not only the Congo crisis but the beginnings of military coups in a large number of states. Since I was lecturing on and writing about the contemporary scene, I was called upon to explain these multiple new happenings. I came to feel that I was chasing headlines, and that this was not the proper role of a social scientist. During the time that I was doing the field work on the movement for African unity in 1965, I decided to try out a new approach to these issues by expanding the space scope and the time scope of my analyses. I gave three versions of a first cut at this approach at three African universities—Legon in Ghana, Ibadan in Nigeria, and Dar-es-Salaam in Tanzania.

The interested reception led me to try two things when I returned to Columbia. I created a new course that put this expanded scope into the analysis, and I found considerable student response to this approach. At the same time, the department asked Terence Hopkins and me to give a course on the methodology of "comparative analysis," which we turned into a critique of "the comparative study of national societies." We wrote jointly an article assessing past modes of doing such work (Hopkins and Wallerstein 1967).

At the same time, we undertook a big content analysis project, seeking to extract systematically the propositions to be found in the by-then innumerable articles purporting to be comparative in method. We enlisted some twenty graduate students as our readers (in a dozen languages) and asked them to fill in a schedule about each article we had devised. We never published this gigantic content analysis because we discovered that an extremely large proportion of articles that were "comparative" according to their titles compared one somewhat "exotic" country with the one in which the authors had been raised (usually the United States). Unfortunately, too many authors compared the data they collected in the exotic country with the remembered or imagined (but not empirically examined) reality of their own. Something, we thought, was very wrong.

At about this time I discovered some wonderful articles by Marian Małowist while roaming through *Africana Bulletin,* an obscure journal of Polish Africanists. Małowist was an economic historian of the fourteenth through seventeenth centuries. He wrote primarily about eastern Europe but he wandered afield to write both about colonial expansion and about the gold trade in the fourteenth and fifteenth centuries between the west coast of Africa and North Africa (Małowist 1964, 1966). The articles had two merits in terms of my further development. They led me to Małowist's other writings. And in the first article, Małowist introduced me to Fernand Braudel's great work on *The Mediterranean* (1949, 1966).[4]

It was at this point that my dissatisfaction with the comparative study of national societies combined with my discovery, via Braudel, of the sixteenth-century world inspired a bad idea that serendipitously turned my work around and pointed it toward world-systems analysis. Since I, along with many others, had been describing African and other postcolonial states as "new nations," I said to myself that this must mean that there are "old nations." And old nations must at one time have been new nations. So I decided to investigate how old nations (essentially western Europe) had behaved when they were new nations, that is, in the sixteenth century. This was a bad idea, as it was based on premises of modernization theory, which I was later to reject so strongly (Wallerstein 1976a). Western European states in the sixteenth century were in no way parallel to Third World states in the twentieth century.

Fortunately, I was reading both Braudel and Małowist.[5] What I discovered in Braudel were two concepts that have been central to my work ever since: the concept of the world-economy and the concept of the *longue durée*. What I discovered in Małowist (and then of course in other Polish and Hungarian authors) was the role of eastern Europe as an emergent periphery of the European world-economy in the sixteenth century. I should elaborate on these three discoveries.

What Braudel did in *The Mediterranean* was to raise the issue of the unit of analysis. He insisted that the Mediterranean world was a "world-economy." He got this term from its use in the 1920s by a German geographer, Fritz Rörig, who spoke of *Weltwirtschaft*. Braudel translated this term not as *économie mondiale* but as *économie-monde*. As both he and I were to make explicit many years later, this distinction was crucial: between *économie mondiale*, meaning the "economy *of the* world," and *économie-monde*, meaning an "economy *that is a* world" (Braudel 1984, chap. 1, esp. 21–24). The difference was first of all conceptual. In the latter formulation, the world is not a reified entity that is there, and within which an economy is constructed; rather, the economic relationships are defining the boundaries of the social world. The second difference was geographic. In the first usage, "world" equals the globe; in the second usage, "world" means only a large geographic space (within which many states are located), which, however, can be and usually is less extensive than the globe (but also can encompass the entire globe).

I faced one problem immediately. The Romance languages permit this distinction easily, by using an adjectival noun in place of a true adjective (that is, *économie-monde* as opposed to *économie mondiale*). German doesn't permit the distinction at all orthographically, because one can only use the adjectival noun, which is attached to the noun it is modifying to form a single word. This is why Rörig's usage, which could only be understood contextually, never really received notice. English as a language is orthographically in-between. I could translate Braudel's term by inserting a hyphen (thus "world-economy" instead of "world economy"), the hyphen turning the adjective into an adjectival noun and indicating the indissolubility of the two words, which represent thereby a single concept (Wallerstein 1991b).

I then took Braudel's concept of the "world-economy" and combined it with Polanyi's notion that there were three modes of economic behavior, which Polanyi had called reciprocity, redistribution, and exchange (Polanyi 1957, chap. 4; 1967, 1977). I decided that reciprocity referred to what I called minisystems (that is, small systems that were not world-systems), and that reciprocity and exchange referred to what I called the two varieties of world-systems, world-empires and world-economies.[6] I then argued that the modern world-system was a capitalist world-economy, that capitalism could exist only within the framework of a world-economy, and that a world-economy could operate only on capitalist principles. I make this case throughout my writings. The earliest (and most widely read) version of this argument is found in "The Rise and Demise of the World-Capitalist System: Concepts for Comparative Analysis" (Wallerstein 1974b).

I faced a second problem in orthographics. Both Braudel and I believed that world-economies were organic structures that had lives—beginnings and ends. Therefore, there had to have been multiple world-economies (and of course multiple world-empires) in the history of humankind. Thus I became careful to speak not of world-system analysis but of world-system*s* analysis. This may seem obvious, except that it would become the cornerstone of a fierce attack in the 1990s by Andre Gunder Frank, who argued that there had only ever been one world system and that it had been covering the Euroasiatic ecumene for twenty-five hundred years at least and the entire world for the past five hundred (hence no need for either a hyphen or a plural). Obviously, Frank was using different criteria to define the boundaries of a system. Along with these different criteria came the assertion that the concept of capitalism was irrelevant to the discussion (it had either always or never existed).[7]

If the appropriate unit of analysis of the modern world is that of a world-system, and if there had been multiple world-systems in human history, then Braudel's concept of multiple social temporalities became immediately central. Braudel had built *The Mediterranean* (1949) around an elementary architecture. He would tell the story three times in terms of three temporalities, the short-term, the middle-term, and the long-term. It was only later, however, in 1958, that he explicitly theorized this fundamental decision, in his famous article entitled "History and the Social Sciences: The *longue durée.*"

In this article Braudel writes not of three temporalities, as we might expect, but rather of four, adding the "*very* long term." He has conceptual names for the four. The short term is *histoire événementielle,* the middle-term is *histoire conjoncturelle,* the long-term is *histoire structurelle.* About the very long-term he says, "If it exists, it must be the time of the sages" (Braudel 1969, 748). There are problems with the translation of each of these terms,[8] but the crucial issue is epistemological. Braudel zeroed in on the fact that, in the past 150 years, the social sciences had seen a split between nomothetic and idiographic modes of knowing, the so-called *Methodenstreit*. He identified this as the split between those who looked only at the eternal truths of social reality (the very long-term) and those who thought that everything was particular and therefore nonreplicable (the short-term). Braudel wished to assert that the crucial social temporalities were in fact the other two, and first of all that of the *longue durée*—which harbored structural constraints that have three characteristics: they are not always immediately visible, they are very long-lasting and very slow to change, but they are *not* eternal.

The most immediate impact on me of this Braudelian imperative—about the priorities scholars should give different social temporalities—was in the conception of how I would write *The Modern World-System*. It became not the search for the eternal truths of comparative organizational analysis, which was the norm in post-1945 sociology (including political sociology), but rather the story of a singular phenomenon, the modern world-system, informed by a mode of explanation I was calling world-systems analysis. Braudel called this *histoire pensée*, which may best be translated as "analytic history." Braudel's insistence on multiple social times would later lead me to larger epistemological concerns as well.

What Małowist (and then the larger group of east European historians) did for me was to give flesh to the concept of periphery, as had been initially adumbrated by the Latin American scholars grouped around Raúl Prebisch in the

Economic Commission for Latin America (ECLA). The term "second feudalism," used to describe what took place in Europe "east of the Elbe" in the sixteenth through eighteenth centuries, had long been commonplace. What had not been commonplace, perhaps still is not, was to see that the "second" feudalism was fundamentally different from the "first" feudalism, and that the sharing of a common descriptor had done a great disservice to analytic thought.

Under the "first" feudalism, manorial units produced largely for their own consumption and perhaps for that of surrounding small zones. Under the so-called second feudalism, the estates were producing for sale in distant markets. The view that such units were part and parcel of the emerging capitalist world-economy became one of the fundamental themes of my book, and of world-systems analysis. Furthermore, the view that the so-called second feudalism was a feature of a capitalist system had important implications for the prior theorizing, both by Marxists and by liberals, about the nature of capitalism. For a long time capitalism had been defined using the imagery of nineteenth-century western Europe, of wage workers in factories (often newly proletarianized and not "owning the means of production") receiving wages (which was their entire income) from an employer who was seeking profits in the market. So strong was this imagery that most analysts refused to categorize as capitalist any enterprise organized in any other mode of labor compensation. It followed that most of the world could not be considered capitalist, or rather was said *not yet* to be capitalist.

Rejecting this nineteenth-century view was a crucial step in the development of world-systems analysis. The classic liberal-Marxist view was based on a theory of stages of development that occurred in parallel ways in units of analysis called states (or societies or social formations). It missed what seemed to us the obvious fact that capitalism in fact operated as a system in which there were *multiple* modes of compensating labor, ranging from wage labor, which was very widely used in the richer, more central zones, to various forms of coerced labor very widely used in the poorer, more peripheral zones (and many other varieties in between). If one did one's analysis state by state, as was the classical method, it would be observed that different countries had different modes of compensating labor and analysts could (and did) draw from this the conclusion that one day the poorer zones might replicate the structure of the richer zones. What world-systems analysis suggested was that this differential pattern across the world-economy was exactly what permitted capitalists to pursue the endless accumulation of capital and was what in fact made the richer zones richer (Wallerstein 1979, part 1). It was therefore a defining structural element of the system, not one that was transitional or archaic.

Did I theorize this insight? In a way, yes, but diffidently, although I was sure I was on the right track. When I completed *The Modern World-System*, I realized that it was replete with analytic statements, and that it contained a whole series of architectonic devices, but that they were nowhere systematically laid out. I worried less about the legitimacy of the exercise than about the potential confusion of the reader. So I added a final chapter, which I called a "Theoretical Reprise." This, plus the "Rise and Demise" article (which was largely a critique of the theorizing of others plus an attempt to show how changing a few premises increased the plausibility of the results), constituted my initial theorizing statements in world-systems analysis.

It wasn't enough for my critics. Many reviewers, even some friendly ones,[9] chided me for insufficiently explicit theorizing—I believe the term is "disprovable hypotheses"—and argued that without it my effort was at most interesting narrative.[10] I was also chided for excessively long footnotes, "winding around the page." To me the long footnotes reflected a deliberate strategy of building my analysis around scholarly discussions on empirical issues, attempting to show how recasting the issues (theorizing?) inserted clarity into what had become for most people murky debates.[11]

I should note that not all the criticism was about the absence of theorizing. There were also important debates about empirical issues. Was Russia really an "external arena" in the sixteenth century, as I asserted, or was it rather a "peripheral zone" just like Poland (Nolte 1982)? How could I have ignored the Ottoman Empire in the analysis of Charles V and his difficulties in constructing a world-empire? Was the Ottoman Empire really "external" to the European world-economy?[12] While I was ready to defend my empirical choices, such criticisms raised definitional (and therefore theoretical) problems. In defending my position, I was forced to refine it.

There were two kinds of fundamental theoretical attacks. One argued from a Marxist stance that I had grossly understated the fundamental importance of the class struggle and defined capitalism incorrectly. This was the Brenner critique, which suggested that my view had a "market" bias (sometimes called "circulationism") rather than being a properly "class-based" view of capitalism.[13] In his article, which was widely read and discussed, Brenner had attacked not only me but Paul Sweezy and Andre Gunder Frank as well. The three of us decided that we would not reply either jointly or separately. I decided to take another path in response to Brenner, whose views struck a resonant note among many persons.

A second fundamental critique came from what might be called the Otto Hintze camp. Both Theda Skocpol and Aristide Zolberg launched polemics arguing that world-systems analysis puts into a single arena political and economic phenomena, while analytically they were separate and operated on separate and sometimes contradictory premises.[14] They were right about what I had done, of course, but I did not consider this an error but a theoretical virtue. The Skocpol and Zolberg articles also were widely read.

My substantive answer to both theoretical critiques can be found in volume 2 of *The Modern World-System,* which bore the subtitle *Mercantilism and the Consolidation of the World-Economy, 1600–1750.* I sought to show in it that, against Brenner's version of Marxism, there were not multiple forms of capitalism—mercantile, industrial, financial—but rather that these referred to alternate ways for capitalists to make profits, which were better or worse for particular capitalists according to conjunctural shifts in the operations of the world-economy. Furthermore, I argued that the itinerary of Dutch hegemony incarnated a necessary sequence. It was made possible by first achieving supremacy (in terms of efficiency) in productive activities, which led to supremacy in commercial activities, which then led to supremacy in the financial arena; and that the decline of the Dutch followed the same sequence. As for the supposed separate logics of the market and the state, I sought to show that, on the contrary, a singular logic operated in the world-system as a whole and in all of its parts—the core zones, the periphery, and the semiperiphery (whether rising or declining).[15]

What I was also trying to do, as a matter of tactics, became clear to me. Each volume and each chapter of the succeeding volumes was moving forward in time, discussing new empirical issues and raising further elements of an architectonic scheme. One cannot discuss everything at once. And how all the pieces fit together becomes clear (or clearer) only as one works through the complex empirical data. Furthermore, I had decided on a tactic of overlapping time segments. The second volume starts in 1600, whereas the first ended in 1640, and the third starts in the 1730s, whereas the second ended in 1750. And so it will continue to be the case in further volumes. In addition, the chapters within the books had each their own chronological limits, sometimes violating those of the overall book. This is because I came to believe firmly that chronological limits, always difficult to set, are a function of the problem being discussed. The same event belongs in two different chronological limits, depending on the issue. Writing a complex story requires an intelligently flexible schema.

By now I was also writing a large series of articles, published all over the place. If one wishes in an article (or talk) both to argue the case for world-systems analysis and to discuss a specific issue, one has to balance the presentation between fundamental premises and particulars of the case. I tried to make each important article say at least something worth saying that I had not said before. But I had of course also to repeat much of what I had already said, or the audience/readers might not be able to follow my reasoning. Grouping these articles together in collections had the virtue not merely of making them more available but of elaborating the theoretical skein.

In the early 1980s, I was asked to give a series of lectures at the University of Hawaii. At the same time, a French publisher asked me to do a short book on "capitalism." I replied that I would write such a book, provided I could call it "*historical* capitalism." The adjective was crucial to me, since I wanted to argue that there was no point in defining in our heads what capitalism is and then looking around to see if it was there. Rather, I suggested we should look at how this system actually worked. Furthermore, I wanted to argue that there has only ever been *one* capitalist system, since the only valid unit of analysis was the world-system, and only one world-economy survived long enough to institutionalize a capitalist system. This is, of course, the same issue as that discussed above in my rejection of wage labor as the defining feature of a capitalist system. Is the system a *world*-system or are there as many capitalist systems as there are states?

So I gave the lectures at Hawaii on "historical capitalism" and revised them into a short book. Despite its title, the book has very little empirical historical data in it. It is a series of analytical statements, assertions about how the system has worked historically, and why. Twelve years later, I was asked to give another series of lectures at the Chinese University of Hong Kong, and I used that occasion to make an overall assessment of the capitalist world-system over its history. I called these lectures "Capitalist Civilization," and there now exists a book in print that puts the two sets of lectures together (1995b). This book is the closest effort I have ever made to what might pass as systematic theorizing. It is not possible here to summarize the book, but it is the only place in which I tried to cover the whole range of issues I had discussed in other books and essays, and I did try to show how the various parts of the whole fit together.

In 1976 I went to Binghamton University to join my collaborator, Terence Hopkins. We established the Fernand Braudel Center for the Study of Economies, Historical Systems, and Civilizations (FBC),[16] of which I have been the director ever since. There are three things to note about the center: its name, its mode of operation, and its substantive activities.

The use of Braudel's name was intended to indicate our commitment to the study of the *longue durée,* that is, of long-term, large-scale social change. But the rest of the name was a modification of the subtitle of the journal *Annales.* Its subtitle (at the time) was *E.S.C.,* standing for "economies, societies, and civilizations," all in plural form. We changed, however, "societies" to "historical systems." This was a deliberate theoretical stance. The term "society"—fundamental to general sociological orientations (Merton 1957, 87–89)—seemed to us to have led social science in a seriously mistaken direction. In practice, the boundaries of the term "society" have been determined by the adjective placed before it. In the modern world, these adjectives are virtually always the names of states—Dutch society, Brazilian society, and so forth. So the term required that the unit of analysis be state-structured, thereby extending present-day states into their (presumed) historical past. German society was to be seen as the society of the "Germanic peoples" over perhaps two thousand years, although the state itself came into existence only in 1871, and then only within boundaries that were contested and were to change several times thereafter.[17] We insisted instead on the term "historical system," by which we meant an entity that was simultaneously systemic (with boundaries and mechanisms or rules of functioning) and historical (since it began at some point, evolved over time, and eventually came into crisis and ceased to exist). The term "historical system" involved for us a more precise specification of the concept of the *longue durée.*

The mode of operation of the FBC was somewhat unusual. It involved an organizational shift that reflected a further theoretical stance. Almost all organized research has been done in one of two ways. One mode is the research program of one (or sometimes several) individuals, either alone or using assistants who are hierarchically subordinate and whose intellectual function is to carry out assigned tasks. Using assistants is simply the expanded version of the functioning of the isolated scholar. The second is the collaborative format, in which several (even very many) scholars (or research institutes) work together (perhaps under the leadership of one person) on a common problem. The outcome is typically a work of many chapters, individually written, to which someone writes an introduction attempting to show how they fit together.

The FBC sought to institutionalize not collaborative research but collective, unitary research. The mode was to bring together a potential group around a common concern "coordinated" by one or several persons. These groups are called Research Working Groups (RWGs). Each group spends a considerable amount of time defining the research problem and developing a research strategy, at which point the group assigns to its members research tasks. Assignment makes it different from the collaborative project. The assignment process is collective and not hierarchical. Researchers report regularly to the group, which criticizes their work and sends them out with new group-defined tasks. The results of such work are thus not collections of individual papers but an integrated book written by many hands designed to be read as a monograph.[18] As should be immediately obvious, this approach is the concrete application of the stance advocated in this essay toward theorizing—the avoidance of premature closure.

In addition, this approach was combined with the assumption that addressing complex intellectual problems requires multiple hands and multiple skills. More than that, these problems require multiple founts of social knowledge, drawn from the multiple social biographies of the participants. It should be noted that typically such RWGs at the Fernand Braudel Center were composed of researchers from across the globe who knew many languages, a crucial element in accumulating multiple kinds of knowledge, including those buried in the unconscious psyches of the researchers.

As for the substantive activities, the RWGs have over the years engaged in research on a wide series of major areas that the logic of world-systems analysis suggested needed exploring. And exploration is the key word. Each of the topics was big. Each had enormous problems of locating, in effect creating, appropriate data. Each resulted in a small step forward in the specification of the integrated theoretical architecture we hoped to build. None contained carefully delineated disprovable hypotheses. Rather, each contained somewhat novel conceptualization and used incomplete and inadequate data (but the best we have presently at our disposition, or at least so we believed). And each sought to rewrite the received canons of presumed theoretical knowledge.

Not every group succeeded even that far. Some research projects had to be abandoned. But those carried through to completion and published included the relationship of cyclical rhythms and secular trends of the world-system; the functioning of transnational commodity chains; hegemony and rivalry in the interstate system; regionality and the semiperiphery; incorporation of the external arena and consequent peripheralization; patterns of antisystemic movements; creating and transforming households; the tension between racism-sexism and universalism; the historical origins and development of social science; the trajectory of the world-system, 1945–2025; the origins of the two cultures and challenges to the epistemology; and, currently, a massive project on what others call globalization but what we perceive as "crisis, stability, or transformation?"[19] Each project typically required three to ten years of collective work.

The FBC, like other research institutes, constantly sought funds to permit its operation, and therefore submitted projects to multiple foundations. We discovered that when we applied to the NSF or even to the NEH, we typically received outside evaluations that were evenly balanced between enthusiasm and deep skepticism. Few reviewers seemed neutral. Sometimes we got the money and sometimes we did not. But the deep skepticism would always center on methodological questions, on the degree to which the research method we suggested was insufficiently positivist and therefore, in the view of some reviewers, insufficiently scientific. We realized some twenty years ago that if one wished to reconstruct the way the analysis of the contemporary world was done, it was insufficient to present data, or even to present data undergirded by a solid theoretical explanation. We had to tackle the question of how one knows what one purports to know or, more properly, the appropriate epistemology for social science.

In the 1980s a second challenge to our work came from that broad current some call cultural studies and others postmodernism or post-other things. For these critics, it was not that we had too few disprovable hypotheses but that we had far too many. World-systems analysis was said to be just one more "grand narrative" to be cast into the dustbin, however recently it had been constructed. We may have been under the illusion that we were challenging the status quo of world social science; for these critics we incarnated that status quo. We were said to have committed the fatal sin of ignoring culture.[20]

I turned my attention to these issues, as did the Fernand Braudel Center. I could argue that this was just a matter of our unfolding agenda (one can't do everything at the same time), but no doubt the pace of one's agenda increases when one's feet are to the fire. I suppose it was therefore fortunate (but then, there are really no accidents in intellectual history) that it was at this time that I discovered Ilya Prigogine. I had never even heard of him, but when I heard him speak at a conference in 1981 I was amazed to hear someone formulate so clearly what I had long been feeling in a confused fashion. And to find that this someone had a Nobel Prize in chemistry was, to say the least, astonishing to me at the time.

Prigogine is a chemist by training. The historical relationship of chemists to physicists is one in which the physicists reproached the chemists for being insufficiently Newtonian, that is, for being insufficiently positivist. Chemists were constantly describing phenomena, such as the second law of thermodynamics, in ways that seemed to contradict the premises of classical dynamics—for example, by seeming to deny time-reversibility. Physicists argued that these descriptions/laws must be considered interim formulations, essentially the result of incomplete knowledge, and that eventually what the chemists were analyzing would come to be described in more purely Newtonian terms. Prigogine received his Nobel Prize in 1977 for his work on "dissipative processes" but more generally in fact for being a leader in the analysis of the physics of non-equilibrium processes, central to the emerging large field of "complexity studies." What is more, as he continued his work, Prigogine got bolder. He was no longer merely saying that non-equilibrium processes exist *in addition to* equilibrium processes. He began to say quite clearly that equilibrium processes are a very special, an *unusual* case, of physical reality, and that this can be demonstrated in the heartland of classical physics itself, dynamical systems.[21]

I shall not review the details of his arguments here.[22] What became central for my own analysis, and in my opinion for social science as a whole, are two interrelated elements of the Prigogine construct. The first is the fundamental indeterminacy of all reality—physical and therefore social. One should be clear about what one means by indeterminacy. It is *not* the position that order and explanation do not exist. Prigogine believes that reality exists in a mode of "deterministic chaos." That is, he takes the position that order always exists *for a while*, but then inevitably undoes itself when its curves reach points of "bifurcation" (that is, points where there are two equally valid solutions for the equations), and that the choice actually made in a bifurcation *intrinsically* cannot be determined in advance. It is not a matter of our incomplete knowledge but of the *impossibility* of foreknowledge.

I have since argued that Prigogine's position is the call for an "unexcluded middle" (determined order and inexplicable chaos) and is, in this regard, absolutely parallel to that of Braudel, who also rejects the two extremes presented as the exclusive antinomies of particularism and eternal universals, insists on orders (structural time) that inevitably undo themselves and come to an end (see Chapter 5). Prigogine's position had two consequences for world-systems analysis: one was psychologico-political, and the second was intellectual.

The psychologico-political one is not to be underestimated. Nomothetic social science is based on the absolute legitimacy of the Newtonian verities, as a model and a constraint. To have a physical scientist challenge these verities in a plausible way, and to see this challenge become a central part of a serious and substantial knowledge movement within the physical sciences itself, undermines the intimidating effect, so pervasive within the social sciences, of arguments put forward by those who hold on to outmoded scientific methodologies (for example, methodological individualism) when the physicist progenitors of these methodologies are in the process of rethinking them, or rather (as I have insisted) *unthinking* them, that is, of removing them from our internalized and now subconscious assumptions.[23]

The intellectual consequence is still more important. Prigogine's work has immediate implications for how one does world-systems analysis, and indeed for how one does any kind of social science. It enables one to place precise referents to the concept of the "normal" development of a structure, when the laws of that structure hold and when processes tend to return to equilibrium (what we call the "cyclical rhythms" of the world-system), and to distinguish this period of "normal" development (the development taking the form of "secular trends") from the moments of structural crisis. The moments of structural crisis are those in which the system has moved "far from equilibrium" and is approaching the bifurcation. At that point, one can only predict that the existing system cannot continue to exist, but not which fork it will take. On the other hand, precisely because at a bifurcation the swings of the curve are more violent, every input has more significant impact, the opposite of what happens during "normal" periods, when large inputs result in small amounts of change.

We were now able to take this as a model of transformation of the most complex of all systems, social systems. We could argue, with both Braudel and Prigogine, that such systems have lives—beginnings, normal development, and terminal crises. We could argue that, in terminal crises, the impact of social action was much greater than in periods of normal development. We could call this the period in which "free will" prevails.[24] And we could then apply this to an analysis of the modern world-system. Thus, in the collective work of the Fernand Braudel Center, *The Age of Transition: Trajectory of the World-System, 1945–2025* (1996), we argued, on the basis of an analysis of six vectors of the world-system between 1945 and 1990, that the world-system was in structural crisis and was facing a bifurcation.[25]

Prigogine's second contribution was to insist that time-reversibility was absurd—absurd not only where it seemed obviously absurd, as in heat processes or social processes, but in every aspect of physical reality. He adopted the forgotten slogan of Arthur Eddington, "the arrow of time," and argued the case that even atoms were determined by an arrow of time, not to speak of the universe as a whole. Here too he joined forces with Braudel, and here too it was crucial that this theme was coming from a physical scientist. Of course, it added plausibility to our insistence that social systems were *historical* systems, and that no analysis, at any level, can omit taking into account the arrow of time.[26]

We had been thrust into the maelstrom of epistemological debates, which in the end are philosophical as well as scientific. These issues moved to the center of world-systems analysis. Our contribution was to understand the evolution of these debates as a process of the modern world-system, as an integral reflection of its geoculture. I discussed these issues in *Unthinking Social Science* (2001 [originally 1991]). And in 1993, with a grant from the Gulbenkian Foundation, we set about convening an international commission to study the historical evolution of the social sciences and to look into their possible restructuring.

Constructing the commission was a key part of the task. We decided to keep it small in order that it be workable—hence ten persons. We decided we wanted persons from different disciplines in the social sciences. We decided we also wanted to have some physical scientists, and some persons from the humanities. We ended with quotas of 6-2-2. We also decided we wanted persons from all over the world (all five continents), and from different linguistic traditions (we managed four). With a ten-person limit, we couldn't include everything, but we came close. We also wanted persons who had shown prior interest in the large epistemological issues.[27]

The commission's report, *Open the Social Sciences* (Wallerstein et al. 1996),[28] contains four chapters. The first is on the historical construction of the social sciences from the eighteenth century to 1945. The second deals with three major debates since 1945: the validity of the distinctions among the social sciences; the degree to which the heritage is parochial; and the reality and validity of the distinction between the "two cultures." The third chapter asks, what kind of social science shall we now build? and discusses four issues: humans and nature; the state as an analytic building block; the universal and the particular; and objectivity. The final chapter is a conclusion on restructuring the social sciences.

Aside from the contribution the report tried to make to the understanding of the historical construction and current intellectual dilemmas of the social sciences, it also pointed (albeit in a minor way) to the historical construction of the more enveloping schema, the "two cultures." It seemed to us that the next step for world-systems analysis was to understand how the very categories of knowledge had come into existence, what role such categories played in the operations of the world-system, and how they shaped the emergence of world-systems analysis itself. Here I can only report on a work in progress at the FBC, which has taken as its object of its study just that: the reasons why the distinction between "philosophy" and "science" became so central to modern thought in the eighteenth century, for it is easy to show that before then most thinkers thought the two concepts not only were not antagonistic but overlapped (or were even virtually identical). We are also studying why a series of challenges to this distinction emerged in multiple fields in the post-1945 and especially the post-1970 period. We are trying to tie these challenges to the structural crisis of the world-system (Lee 1996).

In the Giddens-Turner volume of 1987, I wrote an article on "world-systems analysis," calling for a debate about the paradigm. It opens with the sentences: " 'World-systems analysis' is not a theory about the world, or about a part of it. It is a protest against the ways in which social scientific activity was structured for all of us at its inception in the middle of the nineteenth century" (Wallerstein 1987, 309). In 1989 I gave a talk later published as "World-Systems Analysis: The Second Phase" (Wallerstein, 1990b). In that article, I outlined a number of unfinished tasks. I said that the key issue, and "the hardest nut to crack" was how to overcome the distinction of three social arenas: the economic, the political, and the sociocultural. I pointed out that even world-systems analysts, even I myself, although we proclaimed loudly the spuriousness of separating the three arenas that are so closely interlinked, nonetheless continued to use the language of the three arenas and seemed unable to escape it. And in a millennium symposium of the *British Journal of Sociology* in 2000, I called for sociologists to move forward to the construction of a new and reunified discipline I call "historical social science" (see Chapter 10).

I continue to believe that world-systems analysis is primarily a protest against the ways in which social science is done, including in the area of theorizing. I continue to believe that we must somehow find modes of description that dismiss the very idea of the separation of the three arenas of social action. I continue to believe that the historic categorizations of the disciplines of the social sciences make no intellectual sense any more. But if we continue to protest, it is because we remain a minority. And if we cannot solve the "key" theoretical conundrum, perhaps we deserve to be. For without solving it, it is hard to convince others of the irrelevance of our consecrated disciplinary categories.

Hence I continue to believe that we are engaged in an uphill battle, but also that this battle is part and parcel of the systemic transformation through which we are living and which will continue for some time yet. Consequently, I continue to believe that our efforts are worthwhile. But we must be open to many voices and many critics if we are to go further. And that is why I continue to believe that it is premature to think of what we are doing as a theory.

PART II

Dilemmas of the Disciplines

7 History in Search of Science

Myth, the presumed structure of the pre-modern or the savage ... mind, was the single belief the enlightened class did not tolerate. Discrediting it seemed vital to the superiority of the modern world view.
  —Vassilis Lambropoulos (1993, 162)

If human activity is the direct product of the gods, then recounting it is a sacred duty and can only be fulfilled by being faithful to the intent of the gods. But if human activity is the total responsibility of humans, then no referential authority is required to recount it, to analyze it, to interpret it. Modern science defined itself as the explanation of the natural as opposed to the magical. Science refused to accept magic as a meaningful category of reality. Magic was an illusion. The fact that people believed in illusions was real and subject to scientific analysis—but only if the scientist rejected *a priori* the validity of magic.

History—or perhaps I should say modern history, history as written in the nineteenth and twentieth centuries—was the child of this scientific passion. History, *wie es eigentlich gewesen ist,* refused to accept revealed truth, speculation, fiction—that is, magic—as meaningful categories of reality. They were illusions. Thus it is that, for two centuries at least, history has been in search of science.

The search has been incessant, and is embedded in the ever-present litany about objectivity. It makes no difference

111

that objectivity was pursued in hypocritical ways (see Novick 1988; also Diamond 1992). The belief in an objective truth that is knowable has been the prevailing doctrine of the world's historians for these two centuries. The basic data used by these historians were the so-called primary documents, that is, documents that for some reason recorded events at the time they occurred, or were in fact the events themselves. Secondary documents were defined as those things that used documents, even primary documents, without being themselves primary documents. Secondary documents were dubious evidence because of the intrusion into the knowledge circuit of a nonparticipant in the event, an intruder whose motives were uncertain. But even seemingly primary documents were suspect. Any such purported document was submitted to a *Quellenkritik,* a verification of the plausibility of its authenticity.

Source criticism was, to be sure, a highly controversial doctrine in historiography. For it was feared by some that source criticism could first of all be applied to the Bible, a document that had long been treated by Europeans as an unimpeachable primary document. And indeed, *Quellenkritik* was applied to the Bible in the form of the "Higher Criticism," whose beginnings occurred alongside the modern historiographical revolution. Historians thus joined natural scientists in their struggle with the churches, at least with any dogmatic and literalist interpretation of revealed truth. It matters not that many noted historians were pious believers. So was Isaac Newton. What matters is the essentially secular, scientistic claim of the historians: there is a real world, which evolves naturally, and its history can be known.

How is it, then, that historians came to be classed for the most part as opponents of science, as part of that other, more literary, "culture" of which C. P. Snow spoke? How is

it that most historians were idiographic rather than nomothetic social scientists? Ironically, the principal motivating
element in their anti-nomothetic stance was their "search
for science." Historians were haunted by their image of philosophy and of what was called the philosophy of history.
They had rebelled against philosophy, which was seen as
deductive, and therefore speculative, and therefore fictional
or magical. In their struggle to liberate themselves from the
social pressures of hagiography, they insisted on being empirical, on locating "sources" of real "events." To be nomothetic
was to "theorize" and therefore to "speculate." It was to be
"subjective," and therefore to go beyond what was knowable
or, worse, to describe reality incorrectly and prejudicially.

Historians observing sociologists or economists at work
saw unjustified (and unjustifiable) leaps of inference in their
generalizations, based usually on few sources, and those
sources dubious at best. The historians tended to generalize
this observation a bit hastily into the observation that all
generalizations about social events were illegitimate because
all events are unique. By definition, history does not repeat
itself. To suggest that it does is to invent fables. We cannot
enter the same water twice.

If the nomothetic social scientists replied to idiographic
historians that all explanation is theoretical and is necessarily based on the assumption that phenomena are categoriz-
able and law-like (that is, repetitive), the idiographic historians tended to retreat to the position that, whereas this
may be true of inert matter, or even of most living organisms, it could not apply to historical research because human
beings were self-conscious actors, hence autonomous and
unpredictable. They argued that the reality of human will
made it impossible to generalize, that is, to predict (or even
postdict) human behavior. In this way historians, in their

search for science, while rejecting philosophy and revealed truth, fell back in the end on the uniqueness of the soul as the underpinning of their epistemology.

The obvious question was, if generalizations were intrinsically impossible, then what was the point of writing history? Logically, there was only one possible answer—empathetic insight. By recreating the story of what happened, the reader is moved to understand another. The justification is aesthetico-moral, akin to what a dramatist would say if one asked what was the point of writing a play. The answer is hermeneutic cathexis. There were those for whom this answer was insufficient, as for example the *Annales* school. The *Annales* historians said that history, to be faithful to its objective of explaining reality, had to set itself questions that required answers (*histoire-problème*) and therefore had to be analytic (*histoire pensée*). Given such a definition, these historians were less reluctant to admit their scientific ethos, even if they never renounced narrative and style as intrinsic elements of their craft.

The battle between empiricist/positivist/idiographic historians and analytic/social scientific historians has been spectacular. I wish to argue that nonetheless the epistemological gap between the two camps, while real, has been much narrower than its proponents have argued. Both schools, not just one of them, were "in search of science." It suffices to notice that the presumably more "humanistic" (and ergo supposedly anti-scientistic) camp has regularly been called "positivist," a term of scientific or scientistic jargon.

Both schools were equally engaged in "interpretation," if by that we mean the search for realities below the surface, the search for meanings that are somehow hidden. The real difference between the long dominant "positivist" mainstream of modern historiography and the "anti-Establishment" analytic historians was not whether or not one should interpret, but whether the hidden intents for which one seeks are those of individual motivations or those of collective, even objective, forces. This is no doubt a real debate, but it is not a debate centered around a presumed difference between humanism and science.

Nonetheless, if one spoke to historians, if one speaks to them today, we shall discover that many of them, perhaps even most of them, believe in the reality of the two cultures and in the fact that writing history and doing science are distinct kinds of activity. These historians would be surprised at the assertion that they were "in search of science." The reason is that they have misperceived the essence of science as a human activity. However, if historians have misperceived the essence of science as a human activity, it is primarily because natural scientists have misperceived and misstated their own activity. Scientists have created deceptive, self-serving mythologies.

The self-deception of science has been going on for centuries. But it is finally changing. This is what we mean by the "new science." The new science seems to me first of all an attack on the *mythologies* of traditional (that is, Newtonian/Baconian/Cartesian) science. The new science (see Lee 1992) does not suggest that equilibria and linearity do not exist. It suggests that they are not the statistically dominant expression of reality, that they are infrequent, that they are special cases, and that the indeterminacy of bifurcations is a central reality with which we must cope. The new science does not say mathematical calculations are irrelevant. It raises the question whether the relentless quest for precision may not prevent us from obtaining measures that are more meaningful, stable, and realistic. The new science has not renounced the view that the description of reality is not to be ordained by any authority and is always subject to empirical verification. But it has renounced the theoretical possibility of the neutral observer, both because the observation always changes the reality (often importantly, as in the Heisenberg uncertainty principle), and because the theoretical frameworks with which reality is observed are social constructions subject to social revision (as in Kuhnian paradigms). The new science is at least aware that there is a social history to truth, and that scientific advance depends heavily on the faith with which we endow the claims of the community of scientific practitioners (see Shapin 1994).

Above all, the new science emphasizes the constant complexification of reality through the arrow of time and calls upon us to organize our research around these premises. This is good news for historians, for it means that, in their search for science, they have finally encountered a mode of scientific analysis that resonates deeply with what they want to be doing. They have finally encountered a science that makes the quarrel of idiographic versus nomothetic epistemologies irrelevant. They have finally encountered a natural science that is a history. Whether henceforth we call natural science history or history natural science is a matter of sentiment and convention, a small semantic bubble.

I make no claims to judge what are today the best and most interesting problems to pursue or the most useful techniques to use for students of, say, molecular structures. I restrict myself to some suggestions as to where the historical social sciences should be heading. I believe that history must start its quest for science anew. We have to rid ourselves of the assumptions and premises that we incorporated into our mentalities and reified as our *Weltanschauungen* in early modern times, and that we institutionalized as our disciplinary categories and methodologies in the nineteenth century. We must go in search of the new science, as it goes in search of us.

The nineteenth century institutionalized a division of the medieval faculty of philosophy into three main divisions: the natural sciences on the one side, the humanities on the other, with the social sciences sitting uneasily between them as the "third" culture. We are witnessing today a blurring of the meaningfulness of these boundaries, both those between the social and the natural sciences and those between the social sciences and the humanities (see Santos 1992). In addition, within the social sciences, we are seeing a tremendous overlapping, virtually a total imbrication, of the so-called separate disciplines. The solution is distinctly *not* to be found in becoming "multidisciplinary," since multidisciplinarity, far from overcoming the irrationalities of the disciplines, presumes their solidity. Multidisciplinarity builds on sand, for today our "disciplines" are reduced to sand.

The way forward is instead to grapple with the classic antinomies of nineteenth-century thought, show them to be false dilemmas, and seek to go beyond them. Out of this may come a new programmatic division of labor that will allow us more effectively to account for and confront the historical choices before us. I shall discuss three such antinomies—nomothetic/idiographic; fact/value; micro/macro—and then look at the usefulness of our conceptual trinity of social arenas: the market, the state, and society.

The nomothetic/idiographic antinomy of two competing (or, for some, two mutually exclusive) epistemologies is based on the assumptions of Newtonian science, in which TimeSpace is an eternal external parameter, whose values the scientists should always seek to eliminate from the analysis. If this is our starting point, a nomothetic epistemology—the search for covering laws that hold true across all of (real and possible) time and space—is of course indicated. It also then follows that, in practice, the researcher must reduce as much as possible the number of variables taken into account. The resulting simplification is a distortion that leads us immeasurably far from the analysis of real, complex historical systems.

It is here that the idiographic critique enters. The humanist historian has always insisted on the dense texture of real life, the quite visible uniqueness of all describable realities, and the low level of plausibility of the nomothetic recountings of sequences. But, of course, the idiographic critics went from the frying pan into the fire. By insisting on incomparable uniqueness, they made TimeSpace as external to the analysis as had the nomothetic social scientists. By objecting to abstract concepts, they effectively eliminated the vast majority of factors that entered into accounting for the sequences they were depicting. It was another, different, but equally pernicious distortion or simplification.

If we begin, however, with the arrow of time as an intrinsic factor in reality, if we add that TimeSpaces are social creations, if we believe that multiple TimeSpaces coexist in any concrete social situation (see Wallerstein 1993b), then the epistemology that we must use is inevitably an *Aufhebung* of the nomothetic/idiographic antinomy. I call it the concept of historical systems, wherein we recognize that human beings historically have clustered in structures that are discernible realities with real boundaries, if realities that are changing and sometimes difficult to specify. Such historical systems, like all systems, are partially open, partially closed; that is, they have rules by which they operate (they are systemic), and everevolving contours and contradictions (they are historical).

There are of course constant fluctuations in any system that the structures seek to contain; that is, there are cyclical rhythms we can identify, describe, and explain in functional terms. But each rhythmic fluctuation, resolving some short-term difficulty, moves the system in particular directions; that is, there are secular trends. And these secular trends accentuate the contradictions within the system, such that at some point the short-term rhythmic solutions to continuing difficulties become impossible because of the changes wrought by the long-term secular trends. At this point the fluctuations become wilder, and we have a bifurcation, with an indeterminate outcome. Hence historical systems, like all systems, have a bounded history: they come into existence, they live their lives, they come to an end.

For historians, such a model requires that we identify historical systems and then analyze them at the three moments of their historical trajectory. There is first the moment of genesis: how is it that a given historical system came into existence at the time and in the place that it did (and not earlier or later, or elsewhere)? What were the unique complex confluence of variables that can best account for this genesis? There is, second, the long period of historical development: What are the rules by which the system has functioned? What were the constraints that were limiting the fluctuations caused by multiple human activity? The story is always a story of power and resistance, of structures and *conjonctures,* but the weight of the description is with repetition and continuity. And, third, at some point there came the moment of structural crisis and of the difficult transition from a historical system that is collapsing from its "successes" and its "perfections" into its one or more successor systems. This story is one of confusion and uncertainty, and of the large output that small input creates under the special circumstances of a bifurcation.

Techniques that seem congruent with nomothetic analysis will have some utility in analyzing the long period of the historical development of a historical system—provided, to

be sure, that we maintain complexification, rather than simplification, as our objective. But such techniques have little
value if we wish to analyze either the genesis or the period
of crisis of a historical system. In such situations historical
choice moves to the forefront. We are located amid acute,
massive struggles over values that become paramount to
the scientific analysis itself.

We should thus turn our attention to the fact/value
antinomy. The fact/value antinomy has been at the center of
intellectual debates throughout the modern era. It has taken
countless avatars. It was behind the struggle of philosophy
to gain release from the hold of theology. It was in turn
behind the struggle of science to distinguish itself from philosophy. It has been behind all the struggles between a uni-
versalizing versus a particularizing emphasis in social scientific analysis. In the nineteenth century, the rise of science
to become the preeminent form of legitimating knowledge
production represented a transformation of the *Zeitgeist.* Fact
had triumphed over value, so to speak, in the sense that it
had become deeply illegitimate to proclaim that knowledge
production was consciously being directed, indeed ought to
be consciously directed, by one's values. Modernity was presumably incarnated by objective knowledge, and the scholar
was supposed to play the same disinterested role as the
bureaucrats (see Weber 1946, 196–244).

The problem, of course, is that there is no such thing as a
disinterested scholar; there cannot be. Our values are an integral component of our science; in this sense, science is always
philosophy. Values are part of our conceptual apparatuses,
our definitions of problems, our methodologies, and our measuring devices. We can affirm that they are being set aside;
we cannot actually set them aside. What changed in the
nineteenth century was not the triumph of fact over value

but the largely successful attempt to hide the intrusion of values under the veil of universalism. This protective, auto-persuasive veil was so effective that even in such an extreme case as when German Indologists actively and directly served the cause of Nazi ideology, they could do it using all the apparatus of scientific objectivity, using sophisticated historical and philological methods, and affirming their commitment to the scientific ethos (see Pollock 1993, 86–96).

Value neutrality is under severe attack these days, especially from all those who have been writing under the very broad rubric of "cultural studies" (or the various "post" doctrines). To be sure, the various arguments these scholars are making are not as new as their proponents seem to suggest. There is nonetheless a growing number of scholars who worry that the pendulum could swing too far, that "fact" will disappear in the swirl of a multiplicity of competing "value" statements. Here too we need an *Aufhebung*.

The recognition that "value" intrudes everywhere in science does not negate the concept that there is a real world whose reality is knowable. It only reveals the inescapable context for this scientific quest. Now that the natural scientists are beginning to recognize this (or, more accurately, to return to its recognition), historians may feel freer to confront directly its implications. We may start with the observation of Bourdieu: "The 'pure' universe of the 'purest' science is a social domain (*champ*) like any other, with its power relationships and its monopolies, its struggles and its strategies, its interests and its advantages, but one in which these *constants* take on quite specific forms" (Bourdieu 1975, 91). The fact that this is so, however, "in no way condemns us to relativism" (Bourdieu 1975, 116). Quite the contrary! Rather, it inserts the arrow of time directly into historical research itself.

The historian's problem is always to arrive at a plausible interpretation of reality. But interpretation is always propelled by the questions that are haunting the scholar, and the questions that are being asked are the outcome of current social struggles, pressures, and concerns. We will necessarily offer competing interpretations. They are functions of each historian's position in the contemporary situation, his history, and therefore the kind of TimeSpace readings within which he chooses to make his interpretations. *Quellenkritik* can throw doubt on some interpretations, but it is subject to an interpretation of the *Quellenkritik* itself. What it cannot do is create unalterable reality. Analyzing the "social domain" of science can throw doubt on the utility of the interpretation. But it cannot per se negate its validity. We are not in a situation of majority rule, where whatever interpretation is shared by most members of the community of scholars (is it living members or members through all of remembered history?) is truer. Nor are we in a situation of total intellectual anarchy, in which all interpretations are equally meritorious. Plausibility is a social process, therefore a shifting reality, but one based on some interim ground rules. There can be overlapping plausibilities, even contradictory plausibilities, that emerge from the contradictions of the social present.

There is no simple pathway out of the fact/value imbroglio. That is why so many scholars seek to hide their positions under the deeply deceptive micro/macro antinomy. Micro and macro are always relative prefixes on an endless continuum of possibilities. However, for historians and social scientists in general, the predominant usage in modern times is individual/social system, which is sometimes posed in terms of pseudo-causality: agency/structure.

The search for the unit of ultimate reality is part of the old search for simplification. Once we recognize that reality is irreducibly complex, the very notion of a monad is meaning-less. To say that society is composed of individuals tells us no more than that molecules are composed of atoms. It is a restatement of a taxonomy that is definitional, and not an indication of scientific strategy. To say that agents "act" and that structures have no "will" is to beg the question of where we can locate actual processes of decision-making. Surely we have moved beyond a naive mind-body distinction. If the agent's agency is the result of a complex interaction between his physiology, his unconscious, and his social constraints, is it so difficult to accept that a similar set of interacting variables account for collective actions? To assert the reality of struc-tures as determining outcomes no more negates the reality of biographical actions than asserting the reality of psychologi-cal processes negates the reality of physiological processes.

The whole issue is a red herring. In all of explanation we are always dealing with sameness and differences. To assert a sameness we must abstract, that is, eliminate variables that differ in the two elements compared. To assert a difference, we are merely asserting the relevance of these variables to the interpretation. What we do in a particular instance depends totally on what question we believe ought to be addressed. The local/global distinction in social reality is one filled with political meaning. The choice of emphasis by the historian is an intrinsically political choice, and is indeed probably the sin-gle most important issue leading to overt social pressure on the scholar. Judging the reasonableness of any choice brings us right back to the fact/value antinomy.

Finally, we should confront the sacred trinity of human arenas enshrined by nineteenth-century social science: the economic, the political, and the sociocultural. This trinity is clearly and directly derived from liberal ideology and its *a priori* assertion that (at least in the modern world) the market, the state, and (civil) society are autonomous arenas of action following separate logics, and are therefore objects of distinct disciplines. Since liberalism defined this separation as a hallmark of modernity, historians operating within the strict game reserve of the "past" were not pressed to formalize this distinction in the manner of their contemporaneist social science colleagues. In practice, however, idiographic historians gave strong priority to writing "political" history just as they gave strong priority to facts over value, micro over macro, the idiographic over the nomothetic. In so doing, they tacitly accepted the legitimacy of the trinity.

The whole trend of writing in the past twenty-five years—by historians and by other social scientists—has been to ignore in practice the boundaries of these supposedly autonomous arenas, to stress their interpenetration when making interpretations, while at the same time reasserting them theoretically and verbally. It is time to review and renew our vocabulary. If in fact it is more plausible to see these three "arenas" as at most three angles of vision on a single complex reality, then the very vocabulary serves as a constraint on useful analysis. The "trinity" of arenas becomes an outdated taxonomy, sustained by collapsing ideological visions.

This, then, is the set of immediate tasks for historians in search of science. We must be clear about the kind of science for which we are searching. We must elaborate a terminology that will get us beyond the antinomies dear to the nineteenth century—idiographic/nomothetic, fact/value, micro/macro—and dispense with the concept of a trinity of arenas of human action. When we have done this, we shall have cleared away the underbrush. We must then deepen our realization of how different are the multiple social definitions of TimeSpace and use them to re-create interpretive frameworks that are adequate for our present reality.

Of course, doing this depends on our understanding of what our present reality is. I see it as primarily one in which the historical system in which we have been living, the capitalist world-economy, is in crisis and therefore is facing a bifurcation. I have argued this in detail elsewhere (Wallerstein 1994). I see the present intellectual crisis as reflecting the structural crisis of the system. This creates in fact our opportunity as well as our compelling obligation. The construction of a new scientific vision, one that makes central the "re-enchantment of the world" (Prigogine and Stengers, 1979), will be a major element in whether this evolutionary turning point at which we are located will be one for the better or for the worse.

8 Writing History

The problem of writing history can be seen in the very title of the colloquium within which this argument was originally made. It exists in three language versions. In English it is "[Re]constructing the Past." This version indicates an ambivalence between construction and reconstruction, the latter term fitting in more than the former with an evolutionary, cumulative concept of knowledge. In French the title is "Le Passé Composé." No reconstruction here, but the title permits an allusion to grammatical syntax and refers to the verb tense that denotes a past that continues into the present and is not yet completed. In French, this form is distinguished from the preterite, which is sometimes called "le passé historique." In everyday conversation, one normally uses "le passé composé." Finally, in Dutch the title is "Het Verleden als Instrument," a far more structuralist title than the others. I do not know if the organizers of the colloquium had intended this ambiguity deliberately. But it is hard to speak about history, especially these days, unambiguously.

Let me raise still another ambiguity. In English, "story" and "history" are separate words, and the distinction is thought to be not only clear but crucial. But in French and Dutch, "histoire" and "geschiedenis" can have both connotations. Is the distinction less clear in these linguistic traditions? I hesitate to answer. I do notice that the organizers had charged us collectively, at least in the English-language version of their announcement, with the task of conducting "a large-scale meditation on the usefulness and disadvantages of history for life." This seems to me a wise starting point, for it recognizes that what we are about might not necessarily be useful; it might possibly be unuseful, actually disadvantageous, for life.

And a final comment on the title. The colloquium was said to be a "Colloquium on History and Legitimisation." Is the legitimation of something the instrumental goal that was mentioned in the Dutch title? Are we to be very Foucauldian, and assume that all knowledge is primarily an exercise in legitimating power? I am tempted to say, what else could it possibly be? But then it occurs to me that, if this is all that it were, it could not possibly serve its purpose very effectively, since knowledge is most likely to succeed in legitimating power if the people—that is, those who consume this knowledge produced by historians—thought that it had independent truth-value. It would follow that knowledge might be most useful to those in power if it were perceived as being at most only partially responsive to power's beck and call. But of course, on the other hand, it might not be useful at all if it were entirely antagonistic to power. So, from the point of view of those with power, the relation they might want to have with intellectuals purporting to write history is an intricate, mediated, and delicate one.

I propose to discuss what are, what can be, the lines between four kinds of knowledge production: fictional tales, propaganda, journalism, and history as written by persons called historians. And then I wish to relate that to remembering and forgetting, to secrecy and publicity, to advocacy and refutation.

Fictional tales are the earliest knowledge product to which most people are exposed. Children are told stories, or stories are read to them. Such stories convey messages. Parents and other adults consider these messages very important.

There is considerable censorship by adults of what children may hear or read. Most people rate possible stories along a continuum running from taboo subjects to highly undesirable subjects to subjects that are considered innocent to tales with a virtuous moral. The form of such stories may vary, from those that are sweet and charming to those that are frightening or exciting. We frequently assess and reassess the effect of such stories on children and adjust our choices in light of such assessments. Such stories are of course fictional in the sense that a person named Cinderella is not thought by the adults telling it to have actually existed, and the place where the tale occurs cannot be located on a standard map. But the story is also considered to be about some reality—perhaps the existence of mean adults in charge of a child's welfare, perhaps the existence of good adults (fairy godmothers) who counteract the mean adults, perhaps the reality of (or at least the legitimacy of) hope in difficult situations.

Is children's fiction different from fiction that is said to be intended for adults? If we take a work by Balzac or by Dickens, by Dante or by Cervantes, by Shakespeare or by Goethe, we are aware that it is describing a social reality via invented characters. And we evaluate the quality of such works not merely on the basis of the beauty of the language or the emotions cathected but on the ways in which the work leads us to reflect upon this social reality. There are those who claim that such fictional works are more effective in getting the reader to reflect more carefully about the social reality that is being described than a work of social science analyzing the same topic would be. The intent of such a fictional work may well be to legitimate. Surely this was the object of the classic sagas—of the Iliad, of the Bhagavad-Gita. But of course the intent might be, on the contrary, to delegitimate. Or perhaps the intent of the author is irrelevant, since the text may run away from the author, or the reader may take from the work something quite different from that which the author intended.

Now, many authors explicitly deny any social intent. They may say that they tell a tale in order to amuse the reader or to express themselves or indeed merely to earn money. But, once again, the intent of the author may be irrelevant, and we the analysts may come along and say that the fictional work did indeed have the consequence of either legitimating or delegitimating, of either forcing reflection upon the reader or of making such reflection more difficult. Indeed, such analyses of literature are made constantly.

And then there are those works of fiction that use actual historical characters, such as Tolstoy's *War and Peace*. Today, television techniques permit what are called docudramas, in which newsreel shots are interspersed with fictional sequences. Today, more people may in fact acquire their historical knowledge, such as it is, from such historical novels or films than from reading the works of trained historians. Is there any way we can hold the authors of such quasi-historical fictional works to the demands of something called historical objectivity? Should we want to? And what if these authors are recounting history in a way that historians consider quite false? This is not a merely hypothetical question. For example, there is much controversy, at least in the United States, about the role of Oliver Stone, whose films are said by some (but not by others) to falsify history in the expectation of delegitimating power. Or is it in the expectation of legitimating power more subtly, as some allege?

When we come to propaganda, we presumably move beyond fiction. But how far? Propaganda is usually defined as statements that the maker alleges to be factual but that others consider false. Indeed, in some cases the maker of the statement knows them to be false, or at least exaggerated. Propaganda is an exercise in politics, an attempt to sway public opinion in favor of or against some policy. We should remember that the word comes from the practices of the Roman Catholic Church, seeking to propagate the faith. But of course the Church believes the faith to be the truth. Those who are not believers may choose either to refute with other truths the truth propagated by the Church or to ignore (and thereby tolerate) their propagation.

Propaganda in the public sphere of politics is a word we use to condemn the statements of someone on the other side. No political figure these days would say he is engaged in propaganda. He would doubtless refer to his own statements more positively, saying he is engaged in telling his side of the story. Telling one's side of the story has come to be seen as a legitimate activity in the context of the wide acceptance of the belief that in politics there is no absolute truth, that there are "two sides to every story." The Japanese film *Rashomon* illustrated the phenomenon that participants in or witnesses to an event will all have different versions of it. Kurosawa's film showed this so well that the word "Rashomon" has become part of our vocabulary. We all know that the division between "lies" and "truth" is not simply between Goebbels's "big lie" and the unvarnished truth. This line is often less than clear, that there are gradations and gray areas and intermediate possibilities. In the United States we now talk about "putting a spin" on the news, explaining an event in such a way that it places favorable light on the teller or the group he represents. Thus, while we may agree that Tolstoy's *War and Peace* does not exactly or objectively depict history, who would argue that our politicians accurately or objectively represent "the facts"?

Journalism is supposed to represent a much higher degree of truth-value than propaganda. Journalists tend to define themselves as persons who take the statements of various actors, political and otherwise, check these statements against those of opponents, and then recount what they think actually happened, presumably from a more neutral point of view. They are supposed, at least in theory, to be searching out contradictory points of view, weighing them against whatever evidence seems to exist, and drafting an independent version of reality. But of course we know the many problems with this scenario. Some journalists are not free to tell the truth; others are not honest journalists. Even if we exclude these two camps, journalists who are both honest and unconstrained by the authorities may nonetheless not have the access to necessary information, a problem made quite acute by the rapid pace of developments and the compulsion to "report the story." They are supposed to recount what happened yesterday, not fifty or five hundred years ago. This constraint has the advantage that they may actually be able to interview participants, but it has the disadvantage that they lack the time to acquire knowledge, not to speak of perspective.

Thus, as we try to move up the ladder of objectivity, going from fictional tales to propaganda to journalism, we finally reach the level of the historians, that is, those persons who have prided themselves, at least since the so-called historiographic revolution of the nineteenth century, on the fact that they follow Ranke and tell history *wie es eigentlich gewesen ist*. To fulfill this objective, most historians have accepted a set of rules which, it is claimed, will maximize objectivity. They have sought to base their statements on data, which has tended to mean written documents, although in recent years historians have become willing to take other kinds of data into account as well.

Not just any written documents, however! Historians, at least since the nineteenth century, have made a distinction between so-called primary and secondary sources, and have given pride of place to the former. A primary document is one written more or less at the time of the event under discussion. The presumption is that these documents were written for some immediate purpose, and therefore were not written with an eye to their possible uncovering by a historian some centuries later. Primary documents of course may be difficult to understand, because the language and the contextual allusions are those of some past moment. It is assumed therefore that a competent historian will be well immersed in the cultural ambiance of the time, the result of training and considerable general research.

To be sure, reliance on these primary documents at most ensures that the documents themselves were not intended to deceive, or at least that they were only intended to deceive others living at the time. No doubt we have all sorts of problems about this. Perhaps they were truly intended to deceive, and the historian is unable to decipher this. Or even worse, perhaps the documents are fakes, that is, written later and deposited somewhere to make historians believe that they were written at the time. But even after we consider all these issues, there remains the question of the historian's own attitude toward the substantive issues he or she is analyzing. Will the historian bring biases to interpretations of the data? Here, aside from reliance on the ethical exhortations of the community of historians, it is assumed that there is a structural check, that historians are less likely to be emotionally involved in issues of the past than in issues of the present. This was one of the classical arguments for restricting the research of historians to past eras.

We have always known how shaky all these assumptions are. But we have tended to handle the shakiness by denial. In recent years, a large number of scholars have openly challenged the veracity of the knowledge put forward by historians. Some have gone to the end of this road by arguing that veracity is intrinsically impossible, but others simply argue that we should be very cautious in assertions of truth-value, since every analysis involves an interpretation, one that is colored by the social and personal biography of the interpreter and by the pressures of the moment at which the interpretation is being made.

I have engaged thus far in an easy task. I have been illustrating the fact that there is no simple, hard-and-fast line separating fiction from fact, fable from truth. The line between children's tale and professional history is a continuous blur that mixes reality, political argument, and utopian fantasy. Intrepid is the scholar who would engage in some triage between legitimate and illegitimate historiography. But this is easy to show, as I said. It is far from satisfying. For we all rely every day on "reality testing" in our individual attempts to cope with a very real world. And we rely on help from others to make this adequate. Historians are persons engaged in the social task of making plausible interpretations of social reality that, it is hoped, we will all find useful, not only individually but collectively. Why bother, unless we are ready to devote ourselves to designing such plausible interpretations, whatever the difficulties? We have to assume the risk.

So we come to the knotty question, what is a plausible interpretation? Clearly, there is a question of internal coherence, which is the easiest to judge, if not to achieve. I do not have to agree at all with the interpretation of someone else in order to assess whether the internal logic of the argument put forth seems tight or very dubious. And I personally feel free to pay no further attention to arguments that are not coherent. But this is far from sufficient. I have also to feel that the questions being answered by the analysis are important questions. And I need to feel that the unit of analysis is appropriate to the question being answered. And finally I need to feel that no significant factors have been omitted from the analysis. There are, however, no simple criteria, widely agreed upon by most historians or most people, as to what are important questions, what is the appropriate unit of analysis for given questions, and what are the factors that are significant? These are in a sense all *a priori* decisions.

We can do one of two things with *a priori* decisions. We can say that choosing between them is impossible, that they reflect basic philosophical or political options about which we can only agree to disagree. Or we can try to communicate and debate across these philosophical/political divides by analyzing the *a priori* decisions in terms of what Max Weber called "substantive rationality" (*Rationalität materiel*), by which we can only mean analyses that both seem to account for a larger degree of the variance on empirical questions and seek to speak to the principal philosophical/political questions of our times. Perhaps this only pushes the impossible divide back to another, prior level—from a debate about the plausibility of the interpretation of some limited question to a debate about what are the principal philosophical/political questions of our time. But, if so, this is at least a shift that clarifies the underlying discussion and makes it possible for people other than professional historians to enter into it.

Take, for example, the question of memory. In recent years there has been much discussion of memory, of what we remember and ought to remember and what we forget and ought to forget. It is obvious that these are social decisions, and they are constantly being made collectively. Furthermore, the decisions are never permanent. Even if at a given moment we decide we must collectively remember some past reality, thirty years later it is quite possible that we will prefer to forget this same reality. Why then is memory such an issue these days? It is propelled, quite obviously, by recent historical events. The issue was first put forward because of the Nazis' systematic extermination of European Jewry, what has come to be called the Holocaust. It has been argued that it is vital not to forget what happened in order that it not happen again, and that therefore historians should write about and teach this history. This view of the role of historians in creating and preserving collective memory spread rapidly. Armenians have argued that it applies to the 1915 slaughter of Armenians in Turkey. I have in my office a poster created in Argentina shortly after the ouster of the military, which reads in big letters "Nunca mas" and which denounces the disappearances, the torture, the fear, the humiliations, the moral and material misery, the lies, and the silence of the world. Above all, the silence. And we know how the celebration of the bicentennial of the French Revolution reopened the question of appropriate memory in France. Finally, we know how much debate there has been in eastern and central Europe and the former Soviet Union about what is useful and what is disadvantageous to remember.

In October 1998, in South Africa, a five-volume report was published by a body called the Truth and Reconciliation Commission (TRC). This body, chaired by Archbishop Desmond

Tutu, was constituted by the post-apartheid government and charged with elucidating the truth on violations of human rights in the period 1960–94. The TRC decided to link three questions: truth, reconciliation, and amnesty. In order to arrive at "truth," the commission offered the chance of amnesty for crimes to anyone who would recount in detail and publicly what crimes he or she had committed.

The commission said that it found the concept of truth very complex and that it had come up with four different notions of truth: factual or forensic truth, personal or narrative truth, social or "dialogue" truth, and healing or restorative truth (Truth and Reconciliation Commission 1999, 1:110–14). Factual truth was defined more or less as what positivist historians would call truth—"factual, corroborated evidence, . . . obtaining accurate information through reliable (impartial, objective) procedures." The TRC said its findings at this level served to "reduce the number of lies that can be circulated unchallenged in public discourse," and that this was socially useful. It defined personal truth as the truth of victims telling their stories. These stories were "insights into pain" and created a sort of "narrative truth." It was an act of "restoring memory."

Social truth, however, was closest to the goal of the commission. By interaction and debate, the commission sought "to transcend the divisions of the past by listening carefully to the complex motives and perspectives of all those involved." This was seen as "a basis for affirming human dignity and integrity." Finally, healing truth was "the kind of truth that places facts and what they mean within the context of human relationships—both amongst citizens and between the state and its citizens." It was for these reasons that the TRC insisted not merely on knowledge but on acknowledgment. "Acknowledgment is an affirmation that a person's pain is real and worthy of attention. It is thus central to the restoration of the dignity of victims."

Is the report of this commission history or is it a document to be used by historians with all their customary cautions? This is, of course, a question that not only historians have to pose themselves. The four categories of truth the commission used are in fact a modification of the four kinds of truth put forward by Justice Albie Sachs of the constitutional court of South Africa. Sachs is not a historian but a jurist. He is also a militant of the African National Congress who lost his arm in a bomb attack by agents of the apartheid regime and is thus also a victim. Sachs asserts his puzzlement "as a lawyer and a judge" about truth (Sachs 1998, esp. 9–11). He calls factual truth "microscopic truth" and notes this is normally the prime concern of a court of law: "whether a certain person is guilty of wrongfully and intentionally killing another at a particular time and in a particular manner." It is detailed, focused truth. Sachs's second truth he calls "logical truth"—"the generalised truth of propositions, the logic inherent in certain statements . . . arrived at by deductive and inferential processes." Sachs has thus spelled out here the distinction between idiographic truth and nomothetic truth, long the subject of a *Methodenstreit* among social scientists.

Sachs's third truth is "experiential truth," which seems close to the TRC's "personal or narrative truth," but not quite the same. Sachs says he took the name from Mohandas Gandhi's book, *My Experiments with Truth.* He says he came to realize that Gandhi was not experimenting in the sense that a laboratory scientist experiments, but rather that "he was testing himself, not an idea of the world out there." It was an effort to look at one's subjective experience objectively, "in a truly unprejudiced way." Sachs says law courts will hear nothing of this kind of truth. It "embarrasses" them. Should it embarrass historians?

And finally, Sachs talks of dialogical truth, the concept taken over from him by the TRC. It embodies elements of microscopic, experiential, and logical truth, "but it assumes and thrives on the notion of a community of many voices and multiple perspectives. In the case of South Africa, there is no uniquely correct way of describing how the gross violations of human rights took place, there is no single narrator who can claim to have a definitive perspective that must be the right one." Now, this surely is a challenge to Rankean historiography. But note that this is not a postmodernist suggestion that objective truth does not exist. It is rather a suggestion that the road to such truth is through very intensive, often very emotional, dialogue, tempered by careful sifting of the evidence, in order to arrive at a multivoice, multiple-perspective version of the truth.

To remember and to forget, to keep secrets or expose them to public glare, is to advocate and refute. It is a scientific, scholarly decision. It is a political decision. It is a moral decision. And we shall find no rapid consensus today or tomorrow among persons who call themselves historians about which decisions are the correct ones. All scholarship is an activity of the present, of an ever-evolving present. No scholar ever escapes the exigencies of the present. But the present is also the most evanescent of realities, for it is over in an instant. Therefore, all scholarship is about the past, and I firmly believe that all social science should be written in the past tense. History has no special claim to the past, since all science must be historical, in the sense of knowing that reality at any given point in time is the consequence of what happened at previous points in time, including of course all the radical disjunctures that have occurred.

But since the past is infinite in detail, it is beyond the potential ability of anyone ever to take the entire past into account. We make selections; indeed, we make a cascading set of selections. And we have as our best guide to what selections we make the knowledge we need to make sensible historical choices about the future. The first choice we have to make is the unit of analysis we shall use to make our selections. My own preference is very clear. I think we have to make our analyses within the framework of what I call historical systems, units of large-scale, long-term reality and social change that have some systemic quality, that is, have a life governed by some set of processes that we can analyze and that are held together because they comprise a significant and continuing division of labor. All such systems are historical in that they constantly evolve, and all are systems in that they maintain some continuing features. This means two things above all: such historical systems have spatial boundaries, even if these are changing over time. And they have temporal boundaries, that is, they have beginnings, ongoing evolutions, and terminal crises.

I believe, for example, that we are living today in a world-system that I assert to be a "capitalist world-economy." Today this world-system covers the globe. When it originated some five hundred years ago, it covered a relatively small segment of the globe. Why, for example, should we discuss someone like Charles V? I cannot speak for others. To me, Charles V is interesting because he symbolizes a major historical choice made in western Europe in the sixteenth century. At the very beginning of the modern world-system, there were forces that sought to consolidate the nascent capitalist world-economy and forces that sought to transform it into a classical world-empire. This tension has been a continuing one within the modern world-system. Charles V failed in his attempt to create this kind of world-empire. Had he succeeded, we would not have known the modern world as we have seen it. I say this without any moral judgment. I am not at all sure the world is better off for the failure of Charles V. I simply note it as a turning point of some great importance.

Analyzing Charles V reminds us of the unpredictability of historical choice. Systems in crisis come to chaotic periods and bifurcations. Choices are made. Once made, they result in the constitution of new systems, which then have a life of their own, with their cyclical rhythms and their secular trends. At a certain point in their life, when the secular trends lead the system far from equilibrium, the cyclical rhythms are no longer sufficient to maintain the system in reasonable working order, and the system enters into crisis. I believe we are there today in the case of our present system, although I will not argue the case for that now (see Wallerstein 1998b).

Historians have an extra responsibility in times of systemic crisis. To be honest, what historians do in times of the normal functioning of historical social systems does not matter all that much. They may legitimate the system, or regimes. They may try to criticize them. They are likely to be largely ignored, or in any case neglected in favor of the preferences of more powerful forces. A certain amount of objectivity is asked of them, but not too much. Their ability to navigate the shoals of competing demands is very important to them and their self-esteem, no doubt. And it is important up to a point to political authorities. But a historian assessing the role of historians can only be skeptical about the role historians have historically played.

But if indeed we are in systemic crisis today, then the situation is quite different. For, by definition, a system in crisis is quite different from a system that is functioning well:

in the latter, fluctuations are relatively narrow and individual effort is limited in its effect, whereas in the former (a situation of crisis), fluctuations are great and therefore each individual effort has great impact, in the end determining which fork of the bifurcation we shall travel. Suddenly, what historians write becomes very consequential. Suddenly their "truths" affect people's decisions. Suddenly the scientific tasks that are also political and moral tasks loom large. If we now compose or recompose the past, then indeed history is an instrument. *Cui bonō?*

I end with a statement Pierre Chaunu put in the preface to his book on Charles Quint (1973, 15): "This book, *Espagne de Charles Quint,* is not perhaps totally impartial—but what is impartiality? At least, it is an effort to understand, to explain the past by the present and the present by the past in the solidarity of generations who work on our heritage. We have tried to be coherent. We do not hide our sympathies." Historians should heed this call to coherence that does not hide its values and preferences. And historians should assume the task of contributing to dialogic truth.

9 Global Culture(s)
Salvation, Menace, or Myth?

As we all know, "culture" is one of the most ambiguous, most debated words/concepts in the social science lexicon. There is little agreement on what it means or implies. If we add the adjective "global" before culture, we magnify the confusion immensely. The word/concept "society," of course, is just as ambiguous, but at least it is more anodyne. The concept of culture arouses passion. People—ordinary people, extraordinary people, and politicians—often discuss the concept of culture with ferocity. Some famously reach for their revolvers and others man the barricades. Think of the Sokal hoax (*Lingua Franca* 2000; Jeanneret 1998). I shall not try to construct, deconstruct, or reconstruct the concept. I should say I shall not try to do this *again,* because over the past twenty years I have written many an essay on this theme, perhaps too many (Wallerstein 1978, 1988b, 1989, 1990a, 1993a, 1997a, 2003).

There may not be such a thing as global culture, or so we sophisticated analysts of the world cultural scene may say. But there are many, many people around who believe that this hobgoblin truly exists. For some it is a demigod, for others the devil incarnate. But for all these people it seems to be a reality.

Let us start with those who embrace the concept. Every religion that claims to expound universal truth lays down codes of moral behavior that constitute a global culture, in the very simple sense that these religions assert that certain behavior is not merely desirable but also possible for *all* human beings. Religions thus proclaim norms that they insist apply everywhere and at all moments in time. Surely such a proclamation is an assertion of the existence of a global culture. To be sure, these norms are violated, indeed more often than not. But the fact that norms are violated has never invalidated the existence of a culture. On the contrary, the fact that people bother to observe that cultural norms are being violated has usually been invoked as strong empirical evidence for the living meaning of a culture.

Then there are all the secular religious concepts, many of which we associate with the Enlightenment: liberty, individuality, equality, human rights, solidarity. These too are proclaimed as norms that know no boundaries. They too are not said to be not merely desirable but universally possible.

Furthermore, many people are regularly ready to impose these norms—religious or secular—on persons who are unaware of their existence, who refuse to acknowledge their validity, or who simply refuse to observe the prescribed behavior. When the religious authorities do this, we call it an inquisition (in the case of the members of a religious community) or proselytism (when it aims to convert nonmembers). Once upon a time, religious institutions proclaimed proselytism as their prime task. Today they are a bit more discreet, as the result of pressures coming from proponents of contradictory secular norms, such as religious tolerance.

These days the proclaimers of secular norms are the less modest ones. Indeed, in the past two decades they seem to have the most wind in their sails. Their claims usually go under the aegis of a presumed universal norm of human rights.[1] We now have world courts that purport to prosecute persons who violate egregiously what are considered world norms obligatory even for heads of sovereign states. We have organizations that seek to override one presumed universal norm, the sovereignty of states, in the name of other presumed universal norms deriving from natural law, which these organizations claim give them (and all of us) "the right to intervene." One has to presume, of course, that the interveners are defenders of the global culture and practice its obligations themselves.

For a very long time multiple religions have claimed to announce the one (and only) universal truth, which has meant that we have had competing claims for the content of global culture. Such competing claims are not only impossible to reconcile in terms of intellectual argument but have had very noxious social consequences, in that they have led to outbreaks of immense violence. Secular groups outside the religious frameworks have sought to reconcile these conflicts by insisting on a universal norm of supposedly higher priority, the norm of tolerance. Today we have a comparable conflict between competing secular universal norms, most notably that between the primacy of national sovereignty and the primacy of human rights. This competition has also had noxious social consequences. Is there an outside group interested in reconciling this conflict? How can it be reconciled? Can it be reconciled?

A good example is the Balkans imbroglio of the 1990s. Many terrible things occurred. Some of these things were labeled ethnic cleansing and were denounced as genocide, or war crimes, or crimes against humanity. An ad hoc international tribunal to judge such crimes was created. And today a number of political and military figures have been indicted, and some of them have been detained and placed in the custody of the court and some of them have gone to trial. There is now, in addition a new permanent court, the International Criminal Court. The United States, which supported the ad hoc tribunals dealing with human rights violations in the Balkans and in Africa, has announced that it is totally opposed to the creation of a permanent court, since such a court might bring before it U.S. citizens, and notably U.S. military personnel, for alleged violations of universal norms. The U.S. government has suggested that there might be illegitimate political motivations in accusing U.S. citizens, but it has derided the idea that there might be illegitimate political motivations in accusing citizens of Bosnia or Serbia, Rwanda or Sierra Leone.

The political resolution of the question has been, thus far, a function of relative political and military strength. In today's world, those who come from weaker states may be prosecuted. Those who come from stronger states may not be prosecuted. This certainly makes for a clear-cut procedure, but hardly one that is defensible as the implementation of *global* norms.[2]

Now let us look at the other side of the picture. We all know how differently life is lived in different parts of the world, and the degree to which, on a daily basis, people in different areas respond primarily to the demands of their local "culture." The global cultures I have been describing are probably unknown to a sizeable majority of the world's population and scarcely meaningful even to the highly educated minority who are conversant with these assertions of a global culture. This is true even in the very heartland of the defenders of universal norms, the organizations created to proclaim them and sustain them.

Take, for example, the very interesting case of Roman Catholic Archbishop Emmanuel Milingo, formerly holder of the see of Lusaka, Zambia, who in May 2001 married a woman in a ceremony officiated by the Rev. Sun Myung Moon. Rev. Moon asserts he is the messiah fulfilling the salvation that Jesus failed to accomplish. Clearly, Archbishop Milingo, in these actions, was violating the universal norms proclaimed by his Church. Threatened with excommunication by the Vatican, Milingo renounced the marriage three months later. Milingo had already been in trouble at an earlier time because of sanctioning faith healings and exorcisms, and he was forced to resign his see, but at the time he was not excommunicated or even defrocked. His marriage, however, went even further in defying the global culture the Church proclaims. No doubt, in these actions, he was responding to other cultural claims, more local ones, than those of the Church. This is not unusual; what is unusual is that someone so central to the Church's hierarchy would do this so publicly.

In recent years there has been a vigorous repudiation of the concept of global culture, of its very possibility and desirability. This repudiation has located itself within various knowledge movements—deconstruction, postmodernism, postcolonialism, poststructuralism, cultural studies—although of course each of these movements encompasses a wide range of views. The heart of the argument is that the assertion of universal truths, including universal norms, is a "metanarrative" or "master narrative" (that is, a global narrative), which in fact represents merely an ideology of groups who have power in the world-system and therefore has no epistemological validity. I am very sympathetic to the suggestion that various proclaimed universal truths are in fact particularistic ideologies. But saying this still leaves entirely open the question of whether or not universal norms exist. As many have pointed out, few of the critics are ready truly

to exclude *all* universal claims, for that would undermine
their own intellectual and political positions.

One must wonder about the degree to which the critique
of global norms, of metanarratives, is a tactic designed to
demolish "Eurocentrism"—no doubt a worthy objective—in
order to permit a reconstructed universalism, as opposed to
a definitive opposition. Some speak of constructing "counter-
narratives."[3] And there are some who wish to recognize that
"universalism is always historically contingent" (Wallerstein
et al. 1996, 88; see discussion, 85–93) while still acknowledging that the pressure to create an acceptable global culture
is a permanent part of humanity's history. Furthermore, "the
claim to universality, however qualified—universal relevance, universal applicability, universal validity—is inherent
in the justification of all academic disciplines" (48).

We come now to the question, is the concept of global culture salvation, a menace, or a myth? As should be clear, this
is simultaneously an intellectual, a moral, and a political question. One cannot separate the three levels of consideration.

Intellectually, the issues are classic ones. They are the
antinomies between universalism and particularism, between
nomothetic and idiographic epistemologies, between the
global and the local. These binary contrasts are the terms in
which most debates in social science have been conducted
for the past 150 to 200 years. I will not be the first to say that
these are false debates, totally unresolvable in the form in
which they have classically been posed. But I wish to stake
out this position with some firmness. All universalisms are
particular. But there are no particularities that can be
expressed or analyzed outside universalist categories. There
are no constant social realities across all time and space, but
we cannot know any specific social reality except as part of

metanarratives. Global culture is as real or as unreal as any so-called local culture.

My own view is that we can only make sense of social reality by conceiving of the world as composed of historical social systems. These are entities that are substantially self-regarding and self-sufficient, have rules according to which they operate, and above all have lives. They come into existence, they develop according to their rules, and eventually their processes move far from equilibrium, leading to a bifurcation, chaotic oscillations, and finally a resolution into a new order, which means the end of the former historical social system. Thus historical social systems are both systemic (they have rules) and historical (they have lives and evolve). In this sense, our epistemology must be both nomothetic and idiographic, or rather it can be neither.

For a very long time now, most such historical social systems have been world-systems—the word "world" simply referring to a social system that has an axial division of labor and is large enough to encompass multiple "local" cultures. I have been arguing that the modern world-system is one that originated in a part of the globe in the long sixteenth century, expanded to incorporate all the other territories on the earth within its orbit, and has today reached the point of structural crisis, during which it is transforming itself into something other than the capitalist world-economy that it has been. I shall not repeat here the arguments for this basic position (Wallerstein 1974a, 1998b, 2000c).

When even physicists are acknowledging that the presumably *basic* laws of physics change over time, at least "slightly,"[4] how could social scientists imagine that anything else could be true about human social life? As for the other extreme, those who insist that everything is specific, we should always remember that the thickest description we can imagine is necessarily phrased in conceptual and therefore generalizing terminology. What this position implies in terms of our intellectual tasks is that we need to cease arguing about priorities amid these antinomies. If all social life is both systemic and historic, global and local, then social science resembles an Escher drawing in which whether we go up the staircase or down makes no difference, since in either case we shall be on the same staircase going in the same direction. The point is to be conscious of this, and thus to try and sketch the whole staircase in correct detail. The staircase is there, but not, of course, forever.

One must wonder why what seems, to me at least, an obvious epistemological truism not only is not widely asserted but is in fact vigorously contested. As with all cases of resistance to clarity, or what is asserted to be resistance, the only explanation one can offer is an account in terms of consequences, an account that is more plausible than alternative accounts.

One explanation has been offered in the recent efforts to criticize universalisms. Universalisms, it is said, are assertions that defend power positions in the real world. This is quite true. But this is equally true of localisms and particularisms. Indeed, the insistence on either end of the antinomy permits groups controlling structures of knowledge to limit what can conceivably be observed in research, what kind of findings are seen to be plausible and therefore acceptable, and what kind of policy implications can be drawn from this knowledge. They are very powerful tools in the political arena, precisely because they are put forward as intellectual arguments and not as moral ones, and even less as political ones.

The classical epistemological debates freeze our intellectual possibilities, in particular our ability to see the interplay between the intellectual, the moral, and the political aspects

of the structures of knowledge. They therefore make infinitely more difficult, if not impossible, arriving at substantive rationality, and they push us to rely on the ever more
fragile platform of formal rationality (Wallerstein 1996).
Accepting the idea that (social) science cannot be reductionist or essentialist and must aim at plausible interpretations of complex reality is the beginning of the creation of a
social science that addresses simultaneously and inextricably
intellectual, moral, and political questions. Or, as the philosophers of the world have long told us, we must search for
the true, the good, and the beautiful (three avatars of each
other), knowing full well that we shall forever wander
around their uncertain edges.

10 From Sociology to Historical Social Science
Prospects and Obstacles

When we entered the nineteenth century, neither social science nor sociology existed, at least not in institutional form or as terms in intellectual discourse. When we entered the twentieth century, social science was a vague term encompassing a zone of intellectual concern, and sociology was the name of a nascent organized discipline that was beginning to receive official university sanction in a few Western countries. As we entered the twenty-first century, sociology was an organized course of study in most universities of the world, but social science remained a vague term encompassing a zone of intellectual concern.

The golden era of sociology as a discipline probably was that from about 1945 to about 1965, a period during which its scientific tasks seemed clear, its future guaranteed, and its intellectual leaders sure of themselves. This rosy moment did not last. Since 1965 sociologists have scattered along many paths, quite divergent ones. This has created much dismay within sociology about the presumed future of the field and has led as well to much external social critique. As for the views of the intellectual leaders of the field, do any such leaders exist, at least in the sense that they did in the two decades following the Second World War?

151

In a recent article I traced what I claimed was the heritage of sociology as a culture, that is, as a set of premises widely shared by persons who call themselves sociologists. I then proceeded to outline what I thought were the significant challenges to this culture, challenges so extensive that they might require rethinking, indeed unthinking, some of our basic premises (Wallerstein 1999). I believe that, as a result of the changes both in the world-system as we know it and in the world of knowledge, the intellectual questions that we pose ourselves are quite different in the twenty-first century from those we posed ourselves for the previous 150 years at least.

The era in which sociology was born and has lived until recently was suffused with historical optimism, based on widespread confidence in the unlimited virtue and endless future development of technology. It was an era in which intellectuals believed in human progress not only as something that was good in itself but as something that was historically inevitable. No doubt there occurred many disputes about the nature of this earthly paradise toward which we were all said to be heading, but in retrospect these arguments seem quite secondary to the self-confidence, some might say the arrogance, that people felt about the strides they were taking forward. The many questions that sociologists posed centered around two central issues: the origins of the great historical trek the modern world was said to have undertaken, and how human societies could cope with the collateral damage that this trek had wrought.

We were interested in the origins of the great historical trek for a number of reasons. A clear account would not only enable us to explain discrepancies between the fortunes of the developed world and those of the so-called Third World; it could also justify those discrepancies as a necessary part of the process. The self-serving quality of such justification was alleviated somewhat by the theoretical claim that any such discrepancies were temporary, since everyone was destined to move forward eventually to the same desirable end. An intelligent account of the trek might even help us, it was thought, collectively to speed up the process. And, assuredly, it could help us keep our eye on the ball as to where we ought to be heading.

What resulted were alternative "grand narratives." The principal such narrative, the dominant one, was the liberal view of the world, the so-called Whig interpretation of history. In this vision, humanity aspired to live in an individualist free society, which involved minimizing structures of overrule and maximizing variety of choice, thereby enabling all persons to realize their innate talents in a system that rejected the legitimacy of inherited privileges. In this vision, the world was already well on its way to achieving this goal, especially in certain Western countries, but sooner or later all the rest would catch up.

That this liberal vision constituted the self-satisfied view of those with economic and increasingly with social privilege was evident from the beginning. But because the liberal vision insisted that it was universalist in objective and that therefore everyone could potentially benefit, it appealed to more than its progenitors. Sociologists built on this vision to create the concept of modernity, a term that denoted the more recent of two alternatives in a binary conceptualization of the world's social possibilities: contract rather than status, *Gesellschaft* rather than *Gemeinschaft,* organic rather than mechanical solidarity, and so forth. These binary concepts permitted us to create elaborate descriptions of the modern world and the ways in which it was said to differ from "traditional society." Eventually we could engage in much quantitative measurement to elaborate the description. Since the results were built into the concepts, the data seemed to confirm the vision.

There were two primary challenges to the liberal grand narrative. One was conservative, the other radical. The conservative challenge expressed doubts about the inevitability of the liberal vision, and even more about its desirability. There were conservative sociologists, to be sure. But sociology as a field was not very receptive to their message and never gave their theoretical ideas much space. In order to survive in intellectual milieus, conservatives had to renounce their more reactionary instincts and remold their arguments into a version that incorporated an evolutionary process, although to be sure it was one that maintained the desirability and inevitability of hierarchy in the final outcome. Hegelian thought offered a logic on which such an argument could be built, and Hegel's emphasis on the State was compatible with the ever-spreading sense of national identities.

The primary radical challenge came from Marxism, which offered a variant of the liberal vision that was more coherent than the conservative one, but it was also less different from liberalism. Essentially, Marxists laid emphasis on the fact that the present era was not the ultimate but only the penultimate moment in historical progress. This revision of the scenario had important consequences for the analysis of the present ("class conflict") and for political action ("revolution"), but Marxism shared with liberalism the belief in the centrality of a binary conceptualization of the present and of the inevitability of progress.

The second major concern of sociologists was with the collateral damage of the march toward progress. Everyone seemed to agree that in the shift from premodernity to modernity (however these terms were defined), some individuals and groups were often hurt, at least in the short run. They were said to be alienated, or their lives were disrupted, or they had lost their social compass. As a result, they engaged in activities and held attitudes that were "antisocial," again, at least in the short run.

This assumption of generalized disarray, usually described as urban disorder, provided the daily bread and butter of the world's sociologists. They studied deviance, poverty, crime, and all the other "maladies" attributed to the transition from the premodern to the modern era. But since almost everyone assumed that these maladies were historically transitional, they also assumed that they were reparable. The self-image of sociologists as social workers, or as the theorists of social workers, provides a key to the real definition of the activity of sociologists. Indeed, financial sponsors (states, foundations, etc.) were particularly attracted to this concern of sociologists, without which sociologists would have received even less financial support than they did.

The two concerns—the origin of modernity, and the problem of urban disorder—have not at all disappeared from the writings and thinking of the world's sociologists. But these concerns seem a bit quaint today, not least to sociologists themselves. On the one hand, many, perhaps most, sociologists have moved on to "post"-concerns: postindustrialism, postmodernism, postcolonialism. Modernity suddenly seems to be the past, not the present. As for urban disorder, far from disappearing as it was supposed to, it seems to be escalating. And while sociologists have not ceased to be social workers, they have certainly become more circumspect and less sure that any of their remedies will have the intended beneficial effects. The biographical turnabout of James S. Coleman on how to overcome racial differentials in education was an outstanding and salutary lesson.

The buzzword currently used to describe the contemporary situation is "globalization." Personally, I think this term is meaningless as an analytic concept and serves primarily as a term of political exhortation (Wallerstein 2000c). It represents, however, an insistence, which seems to have resonance with both intellectuals and the general public, that something very new is happening these days. This fits it with the syndrome of "post" concepts and coincides with the vague angst that seems to accompany the dawning of a new millennium. It is marvelously symbolic that the dominant Western countries concentrated their angst at the turn of the millennium not on the second coming of Christ, as they did in 1000 A.D., but on the Y2K phenomenon.

The spokespersons of the neoliberal creed—that is, to be blunt, the priests of the ruling classes—screech reassurance about a glorious future. On television we are told that a million new millionaires have emerged in the United States from the computer industry alone. We are not told that the economic polarization of the world-system continues to zoom forward at an amazing pace. The reassurances are no doubt being received with considerable skepticism. The political stability of the world-system, however, is less threatened by the skepticism with which the unwashed masses receive the balderdash that they may each become a millionaire as it is by the fact that these same unwashed masses are no longer sure that the antisystemic movements that have spoken in their name can, or even want to, implement an alternative glorious future.

One major question before us, then, is whether the twenty-first century promises a linear thrust forward of technology and modernity (whether called globalization or postmodernism or whatever) or whether it portends a collapse of the existing world-system. This is a debate about how to interpret the reality within which we live, which may also hide a debate about the reality within which we want to live. But how can we answer such a question? When we entered the twentieth century, there seemed little doubt about how we could answer such questions. Science—by which we meant Newtonian, determinist, linear, time-reversible science—was accepted as the only legitimate mode of responding to such questions. The only alternative to science was thought to be a theological one, and what distinguished modern civilization, it was argued, was the rejection of the relevance of theology for explanations of reality. The good was one domain, and the true was quite another.

What has happened in the past thirty years has been the emergence of a third mode of explanation, neither Newtonian and determinist nor theological. It is the mode of the sciences of complexity, which argue that both phenomena and explanations are complex. Processes are only temporarily linear. They reach points in their history when they bifurcate, become chaotic, and then organize themselves into new systems. And, it is argued, these processes are indeterminate in the sense that their outcomes are intrinsically impossible to predict and are a function of the actual complex historical input during the bifurcation processes. The extent to which we take such propositions seriously affects the way we answer the question of whether we are entering a period of the summum of "modernity" or the moment of its breakdown (and therefore bifurcation).

Today, therefore, we are arguing not only about the descriptive state of the world but about how we can know the descriptive state of the world. It is not an easy argument, and tempers risk becoming frayed. And we may find ourselves in culs-de-sac such as the recent science wars and culture wars. What we need is some calmer reflection about the possibilities and priorities of social thought and about the organization of our scholarly activities. I therefore turn from the purely intellectual questions of what issues we should be addressing and with what tools we should be addressing them (the theoretical and epistemological questions) to how we can best organize ourselves to pursue our work.

The first problem is the oppressive effect of the division of knowledge into the so-called two cultures. This is a theoretical and methodological schema that has dominated the structures of knowledge for the past two centuries and has interfered mightily with the possibilities of intelligent and useful scholarship concerning social realities. It is the consequence of what has been termed the "divorce" between science and philosophy, which occurred more or less definitively in the second half of the eighteenth century.

The two-cultures divide is still very much with us, but it has come under serious attack in the past thirty years for the first time in two centuries. The origin of this questioning of the two-cultures model is not to be found from within the social sciences, no doubt to our shame. It is the result of a pincers movement that was unplanned and that began to be noticed in the 1990s.

On the one side there has arisen within the natural sciences (and mathematics) the so-called sciences of complexity. The ideas the scientists of complexity have put forth are not new. Many of them were adumbrated in the late nineteenth century (notably by Poincaré), but they did not have an organizational impact until the 1970s. Basically, the sciences of complexity have challenged the fundamental model of modern science, sometimes called the Baconian/Cartesian/Newtonian model, which was determinist, reductionist, and linear. The new group argues that this older and dominant model, far from describing the totality of natural phenomena, in fact is descriptive of very special and limited cases. The scientists of complexity invert almost all the premises of Newtonian mechanics, insisting on the "arrow of time" and the "end of certainties." Quite aside from the intellectual debate, what is to be noticed is that the scientists of complexity have now grown to be a significant minority and are steadily gaining ground within the community of natural scientists.

The other side of the pincers is constituted by what have come to be called cultural studies, a movement that originated in the humanities (philosophy, literary studies). Like the sciences of complexity, cultural studies took as their initial target the dominant view within their own camp, in this case those who insisted that there exist aesthetic canons that reflect valid universal judgments about the world of cultural artifacts, which canons have been passed down through the generations. The critics of the concept of canons insist that aesthetic judgments are particularist, not universal, and that they are socially rooted and constantly evolving, reflecting social positions and continuing power struggles. These critics have thereby historicized and relativized the study of "culture." This movement coincided with and was reinforced by the demands of many nondominant groups for recognition within the university system both as objects and as subjects of study—women plus innumerable class, racial, ethnic, and sexual groups socially oppressed and defined as "minorities." Once again, the thing to notice is how important the cultural studies group has become within the faculties of the humanities.

The social sciences have not been unaffected by these two movements—the sciences of complexity and cultural studies. Still, the discussion within the social sciences has largely centered on how to incorporate the new wisdom of, or conversely how to resist, the new heresies. We have not adequately reflected on what these movements are doing to the structures of knowledge as such. The world of knowledge is being transformed from a centrifugal model to a centripetal model. From roughly 1850 to around 1970, the world university system had separate faculties of the natural sciences and of humanities pulling epistemologically in opposite directions, with the social sciences located between the two and pulled apart by these two strong forces.

Today we have scientists of complexity using language more consonant with the discourse of social science (the arrow of time) and advocates of cultural studies doing the same (social rootedness of values and aesthetic judgments). Both these groups are growing in strength. The model is becoming centripetal in the sense that the two extremes (science and the humanities) are moving in the direction of the center (social science), and to some degree are doing so on the center's terms.

For those of us who think that the two-cultures metaphor has been an intellectual disaster, this is a moment of joy but also of great responsibility. For while it can be said, from an Olympian perspective, that the sciences and the humanities are each moving in the direction of the other, they are doing so amid enormous confusion and, to be sure, in endless variations, some of which turn out to be in fact mere avatars of the old epistemologies they claimed they were abandoning. Perhaps social scientists can help to clarify the issues and thereby promote a new synthesis that will reunify the epistemological bases of the structures of knowledge. Perhaps not, but we shall not know unless we try.

The second issue before us is how to move the concept of substantive rationality into the center of our work. The concept of substantive rationality (*Rationalität materiel*) was put forth by Max Weber in contrast to formal rationality, in order to argue that formal rationality (the optimal means to given ends) was not the only form of rationality. Weber says of substantive rationality that it is "full of ambiguities." He uses the term to mean the application of "certain criteria of ultimate ends, whether they be ethical, political, utilitarian, hedonistic, feudal (*ständisch*), egalitarian, or whatever," in order to measure the consequences of economic action in terms of these values.[1]

Weber himself was ambivalent about the relative priority of formal and substantive rationality, as he was ambivalent about the *Methodenstreit*. But, as is typical of so much of Weber's writings, many of his exponents have eliminated the ambiguities and misappropriated his views for political ends. Weber calls upon us in his final essays to operate on the ethics of responsibility, and it would seem to follow that we must analyze and underline the outcomes of social action and not merely the intentions or the means used. As the concept of formal rationality dissolved in the latter half of the twentieth century into a dubiously universal criterion of highly subjective choices, and as we have come to discover that beneath every choice lurks someone's value preferences, the tables have begun to turn. Instead of formal rationality representing objective reality and substantive rationality subjective preferences, it now seems that we shall have to search for what is trans-subjective within substantive rationality, if we are to seek it anywhere.

It is not that anyone can decree what is substantively rational, and this question certainly cannot be adjudicated by any kind of experimental process. But insofar as we are using the term "rational" to describe something, we must be referring to some process of reflection, and therefore of discussion, debate, relative consensus, and much adjudication, which can bring us closer to defining what is substantively rational.

Far from this being a task for some specialized group of wise (and isolated) philosophers, it should be seen as the central task of social science, which can use its empirical investigations to eliminate implausible alternatives and test the real consequences of proposed paths of action, and can thereby create a sound framework for what in the end remains a metaphysical, that is, a political, debate. However, in a world in which hypothetically the two-cultures divide would have been transcended, this should not have to worry us, much less terrify us. It does mean we have to renounce the naive rhetoric about value-neutral research, and work hard to replace it with a set of operationally plausible constraints on turning scholarship into propaganda.

This brings us to the third organizational problem, the disciplinary categories into which social science was divided in the late nineteenth century. These boundaries are today organizationally very strong at the very same time that they have lost most of their historic intellectual justification. What is happening is very simple. One can draw a curve of the number of intellectual categories into which social science is divided, measured for the present moment by the names of university departments (and national and international associations of scholars) as well as by library and bookseller categories. We do not, of course, have similar data for the beginning of this process, say from 1750 on or even from 1850 on. We do have the names of chairs in the major universities. The curve of subdivisions of social science seems to look U-shaped. In the beginning there were a very large number of categories. The process from 1850 to 1950 involved the reduction of this very large group to a very small number. Since 1950 the curve has been rising again, as "new" disciplines became recognized, if not universally, at least in significant segments of the world academic community. I believe this number will continue to increase in the decades to come, and indeed at a more rapid pace.

The concept of separate disciplines only makes sense, however, if the number is small. When the number becomes large, we are really talking at most of areas of scholarly activity that momentarily bring various researchers together. If we "teach" such narrow areas to graduate students, *a fortiori* if we give them doctorates in these restricted fields, we are essentially crippling students' ability to think as social scientists. We are turning them into skilled technicians. Of course, the organizational problem is control of access to employment. But the intellectual result is collective blinkers.

There are three scenarios possible. We continue to patch together the organizational structure of the social sciences, until one day it collapses of its own weight. This seems to be the path we are on now. Perhaps it can continue. I think it is both improbable and implausible to sit back and wait. Or we can expect the intrusion of a *deus ex machina,* more probably multiple *dei ex machina,* to reorganize the social sciences for us. There are in fact candidates for this role, some of them even eager candidates. They are to be found in ministries of education and university administrations. The principal motivation of such bureaucrats would probably be rationalization in order to reduce costs, although they would no doubt clothe this intention in academic pap. What we could expect from their intrusion is a panoply of different results in different institutions, which might further add to the confusion.

The third scenario, perhaps less likely but probably more desirable, is that social scientists themselves take the lead in

reunifying and redividing social science so as to create a
more intelligent division of labor, one that would permit significant intellectual advance in the twenty-first century. I
think such a reunification can be achieved only if we consider that we are all pursuing a singular task, which I call
historical social science. This task must be based on the epistemological assumption that all useful descriptions of social
reality are necessarily both "historical" (that is, they take
into account not only the specificity of the situation but the
continual and endless changes in the structures under
study) and "social scientific" (that is, they search for structural explanations of the *longue durée,* which explanations
are not, however, and cannot be eternal). In short, process
would be at the center of the methodology.

In such a reunified (and eventually redivided) social science, it would not be possible to assume a significant divide
between economic, political, and sociocultural arenas (no
ceteris paribus clauses allowed, even provisionally). And we
would have to be very careful about the "we" and the "other."
Instead of drawing a line between the modern and the pre-
modern, the civilized and the barbaric, the advanced and the
backward (which we continue to do in so many subtle and
not so subtle ways), historical social scientists have to incorporate the tension between the universal and the particular
into the center of their work and subject all zones, all
groups, all strata to the *same* kind of critical analysis.

All of this is easier said than done. It will never be done
unless and until historical social science becomes a truly
global exercise. Today, for obvious economic reasons, the
bulk of social science is done in a small corner, the rich corner, of the globe. This distorts our analysis, and the distortion is structural, not individual. No amount of virtuous
self-discipline on the part of individual scholars will correct

it. It is not a matter of inviting a few more social scientists from Asia or eastern Europe or Latin America to a colloquium or to teach in a Western university. It requires the systematic displacement of funding. It requires that Western scholars, whether they are accomplished scientists or graduate students, enter into contact with the rest of the world, less to teach than to learn. It requires that they feel that they have something to learn, and more than some pious blahblah about "traditional" values. It requires that all social scientists be able to read scholarly work in five to seven languages, so that they are truly aware of the range of knowledge at their disposition. It requires, in short, a genuine social transformation of world social science. I am only moderately optimistic that this might happen in the next twenty-five to fifty years.

The prospects for such a transformation are at best fifty-fifty, and the obstacles are obvious. At the most fundamental level, a transformation of the world of knowledge is intrinsically linked to the process of transformation of the world-system itself. At a more local and personal level, an enormous number of people have vested interests in maintaining the present situation, particularly its worst aspects. Furthermore, many of these people are in gatekeeper positions—and not only in the Western universities. Still, a new millennium has begun. And if that is in no way magic, ritualistically it forces reflection. And I remain enough of a child of the Enlightenment to believe that reflection can be useful and consequential.

11 Anthropology, Sociology, and Other Dubious Disciplines

The so-called disciplines are actually three things simultaneously. They are of course intellectual categories, modes of asserting that there exists a defined field of study with some kind of boundaries, however disputed or fuzzy, and with some agreed modes of legitimate research. In this sense they are social constructs whose origins can be located in the dynamics of the historical system within which they took form, and whose definition (usually asserted or assumed to be eternal) in fact can change over time.

The disciplines are also institutional structures that have taken ever more elaborate form since the late nineteenth century. There are departments in universities with disciplinary names. Students pursue degrees in specific disciplines, and professors have disciplinary titles. There are scholarly journals with disciplinary names. There are library categories, publishers' lists, and bookstore shelvings with disciplinary names. There are prizes and lecture series with disciplinary names. There are national and international associations of scholars with disciplinary names. The disciplines as institutions seem to be everywhere.

Finally, the disciplines are cultures. The scholars who claim membership in a disciplinary grouping share for the most part some common experiences and exposures. They have often read the same "classical" books. There exist well-known traditional debates within each discipline that are often different from those of neighboring disciplines. The disciplines seem to favor certain styles of scholarship over others, and members are rewarded for using the appropriate style. And while the culture can and does change over time, at any given time there are modes of presentation that are more likely to be appreciated by those in one discipline than by those in another. To take a simple example, historians are taught to favor primary sources over secondary sources and therefore to admire archival work. Archival work is not really an important activity in many other social science disciplines. Indeed, the anthropologist who restricts field work to culling what is in archives is unlikely to find a very friendly reception within the disciplinary camp. I think of these attitudes as cultural prejudices, which are difficult to justify intellectually but which are strongly rooted and operate in the real world of interaction among scholars.

As I am making my arguments within the framework of a rubric entitled a "Lecture in Anthropology," I thought it would be appropriate to indulge myself in what I think of, perhaps wrongly, as one of the prejudices of anthropologists. Like historians but unlike most other social scientists, it is not thought amiss, in the field of anthropology, to begin an analysis with anecdotal material, snippets of the micro-worlds in which we all live. And since this occasion is the Sidney W. Mintz Lecture in Anthropology, I shall begin by an anecdote about Sidney W. Mintz.

In the founding year of the Fernand Braudel Center, I invited Sidney W. Mintz to come to Binghamton on February 2, 1977, to talk to a faculty seminar that met under our auspices. He agreed to come. However, I went further. I gave him the title of his talk: "Was the Plantation Slave a Proletarian?" He graciously agreed to talk on that specific subject, and we later published the talk in *Review*.[1] What Mintz did was to survey the actual successive labor processes on Caribbean plantations over several centuries and write a thoughtful, reflective article on the limitations of the traditional ways in which the terms "slave" and "proletarian" were defined "in isolation" from each other. His response to the actual question nonetheless was a cautious one.

There are two things to note about what happened. First of all, I was violating a rather strong academic norm. One may suggest to an invited speaker a thematic area, but it is not considered appropriate to dictate the specific title. Of course I did this deliberately, in order to commit Mintz to speaking to my question. The second thing to note is that this is not a question one normally poses to anthropologists, even less one that anthropologists have often posed to themselves. Can you imagine Malinowski or Lucy Mair answering this question? It was bad enough, they might have thought, that this bizarre Mintz type actually believed that studying plantation slavery was a legitimate task for anthropologists. But to use the term "proletarian" was surely going too far. This is not a term that one normally finds in the canonical texts of the discipline. Economists (certain economists) might use it, historians too, and maybe sociologists. But anthropologists? It implied crossing the line between the West and the rest. And if this line seems now to have lost its salience somewhat in the anthropological community (but has it really?), that was not yet true in 1977.

My second anecdote is briefer. It concerns Hugh Gusterson, who teaches anthropology at MIT. In an interview in the *New York Times*, Gusterson responded to the question of how he had come to study the folkways and mores of nuclear weapons scientists. He concluded his response by saying, "In 1984, it was unusual to be doing fieldwork in your own culture. If you did it at all, you studied down—ghetto residents, welfare mothers. Nowadays, there's a fast-growing field, the anthropology of science" (Dreifus 2002).

My third anecdote concerns a historian. In a review of a recent book by Richard D. E. Burton on violence in Parisian political life between 1789 and 1945, David A. Bell of Johns Hopkins makes the following criticism: "But by posing as an anthropologist—the scientist who stands to the side taking notes as the natives slaughter each other—he also falls into a trap that has ensnared many others: failing to take seriously the reasons for which his subjects believed they were fighting and dying" (Bell 2002, 19).

It is always revealing, if sometimes disconcerting, to know how your colleagues in neighboring departments view you. I shall not take sides in this internecine sniping among the social sciences, but clearly Bell was referring to the different tonalities of the cultures of the two communities, that of the anthropologists and that of the historians. I believe the issue of "taking notes as the natives slaughter each other" has just recently been the focus of a rather passionate debate inside the American Anthropological Association, one that managed to seep through into the non-scholarly media.

All of my anecdotes concern the disciplines as disciplines. What should they embrace as subject matter? How should we approach the subject matter? Do the lines matter and, if so, for what, and for whom? Let me start by making my basic position clear. I believe three things. One, I believe that the social construction of the disciplines as intellectual arenas that was made in the nineteenth century has outlived its usefulness and is today a major obstacle to serious intellectual work. Two, I believe that the institutional framework of the disciplines remains extremely strong, although I also believe that there are important crevices in the overall structures of knowledge, crevices that are visible at the moment only to those who look for them, which render the solidity of these institutions far less certain than most participants imagine. And finally, I believe that there is richness in each of the disciplinary cultures that should be harvested, stripped of its chaff, and combined (or at least used) in a reconstruction of the social sciences. Let me deal with these three assertions successively.

The Intellectual Justification of the Disciplines

In 1993–95 I chaired an international commission, the Gulbenkian Commission on the Restructuring of the Social Sciences, and we produced a report, *Open the Social Sciences* (Wallerstein et al. 1996).[2] Chapter 1 of that report dealt with "the historical construction of the social sciences, from the eighteenth century to 1945." In it, we argued that the intellectual lines of the surviving disciplines (for one must think of disciplinary names as surviving a culling process that went on for more than a century) fell around three axes: the past (history) versus the present (economics, political science, and sociology); the West (the previous four disciplines) and the rest (anthropology and Oriental studies); and the structuring of the nomothetic Western present around the liberal distinction of the market (economics), the state (political science), and civil society (sociology).

It is easy in the twenty-first century to see the limitations of the presumed axes of distinction. Massive numbers of social scientists began in the last three decades of the twentieth century to disregard these lines in the sand. Furthermore, many persons have sought to redefine the intellectual premises of the various disciplines in order to take into account these realities, and to transform what might have been thought of as academic poaching into legitimate activities. But I can assure you that when I was a graduate student in the 1950s, these nineteenth-century boundaries were not merely in place but very actively asserted and defended within all the disciplines.

What happened? Very simple. The world changed. The United States became a hegemonic power with global responsibilities. The Third World became a political force. And there was a massive expansion worldwide of university education with a consequent massive increase in the number of social scientists doing research and writing books. The first two changes meant that the separation into disciplines for the West and disciplines for the rest became totally untenable. And the third change led to a quest for originality via academic poaching. These days the names of papers given at the annual meetings of social science associations are incredibly similar, except that one adds the heading "anthropology of" or "sociology of" or "history of" to the same substantive phrase.

Do these papers given at different disciplinary conferences read differently? Up to a point they do, which has to do with the "cultures" of the disciplines. But they read less differently than one might think, and certainly a social scientist coming from Mars might wonder whether the degree of difference is worth the fuss. I want, therefore, to play with the following Quixotic idea. Suppose we merged all the existing social science disciplines into one gigantic new faculty to which I would give the name "historical social sciences." I would not include psychology in that mix, for two good reasons. I think the level of analysis is quite distinctive.

And today most (not all) psychologists would prefer to be called biological scientists rather than social scientists. And they would be right, in my judgment, given the kind of work that they are in fact doing.

Now, when the fairy godmother left the room and we found this miracle had occurred, we would immediately feel that this structure was too big and bulky for our own good. Many of us (perhaps most of us) already find the existing departments too diffuse. A merger would compound the problem geometrically. But of course we know what would happen. People would create corners in which they felt comfortable, and sooner or later we would get new subdivisions, perhaps new departments. My guess is that the new departments would probably have quite different names from any we now know. This is what happened when zoology and botany merged into a single department of biology, which occurred in most places somewhere around 1945–55. We now have many, many sub-departments or specialties within biology, but none, to my knowledge, is called botany or zoology.

Let us speculate together what the lines of intellectual division really are in world social science at the present time. I think there exist three main groupings of scholars. There is clearly a large camp of persons who hold on to the classic nomothetic vision, who wish to construct the most general laws possible about social behavior via quasi-experimental designs, using data that is presumably replicable and on the whole as quantitative as possible. They dominate departments of economics these days (in the United States at least, but not only there) and also, increasingly, departments of political science. They are strong in departments of sociology and geography. They can be found as well, albeit in smaller numbers, in departments of history and anthropology. These persons share a lot of fundamental premises and even a lot of methodological preferences. For example, methodological individualism is very popular in this camp. They talk to each other already, and they might be happier to do that full-time.

There is another camp that is in many ways heir to the idiographic tradition. The members of this camp favor dissecting the particular and the different. It is not a question of scale. Although many of them greatly prefer to deal with small-scale phenomena, some of them are quite willing to venture into dissecting rather large-scale phenomena. The point is that their backs go up any time one suggests uniformities. As a result, they are not likely to seek out quantitative data, although they don't all reject such data necessarily in every instance. It's a question of what you do with the data. But they nonetheless use mostly so-called qualitative data. They favor close, almost textual, analyses. They empathize with the objects of their study, but they denounce sympathizing with them, because sympathy is an expression of power. Almost by definition, they talk to each other primarily about what they dislike about what people in the other camps do. But when they present their own work, they find a lot of resistance even in their own camp. They are a quarrelsome bunch. Still, surrounded by the nomothetists, they might wish to escape into their own organizational universe. These people are primarily to be found in departments of anthropology and history and to a growing extent sociology. There are in addition some political scientists, some geographers, and even a few rare economists to add to the aggregation.

And then there are people who feel comfortable in neither of these camps. These are the people who do not deny that they wish to construct grand narratives in order to deal with what they think of as complex social phenomena.

Quite the contrary; they are proud of it. This is actually a quite varied group. In terms of data they are a bit catholic in their tastes, using quantitative or qualitative data as they find them available and plausible. In the construction of these grand narratives, however empirical this group is in its practice and its preferences, its adherents abut on larger philosophical questions, and some of them are quite willing to enter into dialogue with the group who technically define themselves as philosophers. They also abut on large political questions, and some of them enter into dialogue with those political scientists who call themselves specialists in international relations. This group is found all over the place—in history, in sociology, in anthropology, in geography, in economics (especially of course economic history), and in political science—but always as a minority. They too talk to each other already, perhaps even more than the other groups do, this perhaps being a reflex of their belief that they are a persecuted minority.

I would guess that social scientists, left to themselves in a remolded faculty of historical social science (or sciences), might well create three such "disciplines" as intellectual constructs. And I suspect that such a configuration would be an enormous improvement over anything we have now or have had in the past. But will they be left to themselves?

The Institutional Framework of the Disciplines

Disciplines are organizations. They have their turfs, and they have no small number of members who will fight to the death to defend their turfs against Quixotic ideas like those I've just set forth or others that seem to threaten the historic configurations in which the existing organizations find themselves. No amount of purely intellectual argument is likely to sway the majority of the world's social scientists, since these people have "interests" to defend, and since probably the best way to defend them is by preserving the status quo. These people are quite ready to give verbal or even substantive support to multi-, inter-, or transdisciplinary projects, studies, and even degrees. They are ready to do this because multi-, inter-, and trans- all ultimately imply that the existing disciplines have specific and special sets of knowledge which can be pieced together to create a tapestry, if tapestry is what one wants. Ergo, multi-, inter-, and trans- do not undermine the disciplines as organizations. Quite the contrary! They fortify them.

Let me identify what kind of people defend their turf most ferociously. Of course, there is a certain element of ideological choice involved, but I think the issue is primarily generational. The young are sometimes audacious or at least inquisitive and perhaps impulsive. They have to be restrained from wandering off the reservation by the potential sanctions of their elders. The most senior seniors are sometimes reflective, tired of the nonsense they and others have been spouting for, oh, so many years. It is hard to sanction *them*. But it is not hard to ignore them and ship them off into the never-never land of honorifics, where prestige substitutes for power.

No, the villains are those forty to fifty-five years of age, who have become the full professors, chairs of departments, presidents of associations, members of national committees, the juries who award the prizes. They have suffered the ignominies of being junior professors (after the indignities of being graduate students). They have worked hard to make their way up the ranks. They have achieved, most often rightfully, a reputation among their colleagues (not merely locally but nationally and internationally). Can you blame them for not wanting to cast all this aside by abolishing their formal positions and placing themselves in a new unstable boiling pot, in which essentially they would have to fight their way forward again, and without the most familiar tools they have used so successfully? Of course you can't. And they won't do it. There may be a courageous fool or two, but not enough to make a difference. And remember, these are the people with the real power within the disciplinary organizations.

So I have not the slightest expectation that the petty bourgeoisie will commit suicide, as Amilcar Cabral (otherwise the most astute of analysts) hoped would happen in movements of national liberation. No, not at all. They will fight such reforms in every possible way, and there are many ways to do so. And the young and the senior seniors will be no match for them. Nonetheless, the defenders of the status quo will probably lose, for they may find their match. There are two reasons for this.

First of all, the intellectual anomalies are mounting, becoming every day more visible. More visible to whom? For one thing, to the general public. How many times have you read in the newspapers the plaint, what use are economists if they never predict correctly? No matter that this may not be a reasonable complaint. It reflects a delegitimation of the existing work of social scientists. And in the end social science is dependent on being legitimated by the social system of which it is a part. Otherwise there is no respect and no money. And recruitment will in consequence dry up. The fact is that, after 150 years of an amazing amount of work, world social science has much too little to show for itself and is unable to perform the social task that outsiders demand of it—providing wise counsel about how to solve what are considered to be the "problems" of the present.

This perceived failure will sooner or later become a source of major concern to those in the university systems and other structures of knowledge whose function it is to be the link between the academy and the larger social system, and to the money, power, and legitimacy that this larger social system confers on the universities and other structures of knowledge. These people are the administrators—the deans, the presidents of universities, and in most countries the ministries of education. Their job is not to preserve the organizational structure of the separate disciplines but to provide what is considered to be the optimal societal output in the production and reproduction of knowledge. Their job is every bit as political as it is intellectual. We know that almost all such administrators are ex-scholars, most no longer able to devote themselves to serious new work or, often, to keep up too well with the work of others, even in their immediate fields of specialization. Slowly, over the years, they move away from the chains that the disciplinary organizations had imposed on them, even if they are forty to fifty-five.

Let us look at the overall scene from the point of view of such administrators. They perceive the social sciences, on the whole, through unhappy eyes. Social scientists do not bring in a lot of money to the university, certainly not in comparison with the biological and physical sciences. The heyday of their legitimacy is over. The administrators are daily made aware of the degree to which disciplinary overlap exists. And yet, almost every week, someone comes into their office seeking a new center (almost always touted as interdisciplinary), and every other week someone is pushing for a whole new instructional program, even a new formal department. So, while the administrators are dubious about how many such instructional programs they already have, they find themselves besieged by requests for more. And since many of the plaintiffs are playing the game of responding to outside offers, the administrators find that far too often they must yield and permit the creation of yet another epicycle of the social science astronomical map.

Meanwhile, these same administrators are beset by serious, often long-term, economic worries. Of course, the money they have at their disposition varies year by year with the rolling stock exchange. But the question is far larger than this. The world university system expanded at an astonishing rate between 1945 and 1970. But this was a time when the world was economically flush. Some of us call this a Kondratieff A-phase. It came to an end circa 1970, and we have been in a B-phase ever since. The governments of the world have been less flush, but the universities continued to expand, thanks to popular pressure. A larger percentage of high school graduates throughout the world seek to enter the universities each year. They do so because they think this will enhance their life chances, and quite often the governments and entrepreneurs are happy to see them *not* enter the work force yet, given the comparative surfeit of older workers.

More students and less money equals chronic crisis. We have all been living through that. Moreover, there is no reason to think that this economic constraint will go away. True, we may have another A-phase, but we shall also see the ever further expansion of the world university system. For one thing, people are living longer, and hence working longer, all the time, and the authorities of the world-system will try even harder to keep young people out of the job market. Keeping them in the university system is a genuine social solution, but an expensive one.

What would you do if you were a university administrator? I'll tell you what I would do. I would look around to see if I could tighten the ship. One way is to get professors to teach more to more students. This is what I call the "high-school-ization" of the universities, and it is proceeding apace. This of course makes some of the most prestigious professors seek to escape—into permanent research institutions or even corporate research structures. From the point of view of the administrators, this is a loss in prestige but a financial gain. They get rid of some of their most expensive professors.

And then I would begin to merge departments. Why not? They overlap. They don't teach enough. Students are confused by the current situation. A new department with a snazzy title might attract students and at the same time achieve economies of scale. The administrators could even tout it as intellectual audacity. So when I say that the extremely strong organizational structure of the disciplines has cracks that are too little noticed, it is the potential intrusion of the administrators that I have primarily in mind.

Who knows? The administrators might do a wonderful job of reorganization. I have two fears, however. One is that they will be driven more by budgetary than by purely intellectual concerns. After all, administrators are not paid to decide on the optimal ways of defining the tasks of scholars. They are paid to hire good professors and thereby to create a socially useful product. The so-called best universities might be willing to sustain small, unpopular groupings that have some purely long-term intellectual justification, but there will never be too many jobs for those who wish to teach Akkadian language and culture. And reconstructions that are driven by budgetary analyses will too often follow the fads of the moment or the poorly defined needs of the prospective employers of the students.

My second concern is that administrator-generated reconstructions will be done differently in each locality, because local situations are always very specific. And administrators do not have as strong a transnational organizational structure as do scholars in the separate disciplines. The result could be, on a world scale, quite dispersed, and could militate against the emergence of those kinds of institutions that would facilitate the maintenance of world communities of scholars.

This all might well be unfair to administrators, since (as I am arguing) the scholar-teachers are not primed to do such a marvelous job themselves. The point is that we are heading into an era of chaos in the structures of the disciplines and, while I believe that order always emerges out of chaos (to echo Prigogine's title in English), the outcome is intrinsically uncertain (to take up another theme of Prigogine). We will not navigate this era well if we do not cast a sharp eye on what is actually happening.

Harvesting the Cultures of Social Science

Here I enter the most treacherous terrain. My title is an agricultural metaphor, referring to various products of the soil that can then be combined and transformed into useful products—foods, clothing, and everything else we need in everyday life—and which may be better or worse products according to how well we perform the operations, within the constraints imposed by the conditions of the soil.

Perhaps we ought to phrase the processes in terms of a different metaphor, that of the painter mixing his colors in order to produce a work of art on a canvas. I could then list for you my favorite colors, and the combinations that I find interesting or beautiful, and then design for you my picture in the style I find most meaningful. The metaphor of the painter seems to give more autonomy to the subject, who is no doubt constrained by external realities over which he has no or little control, but less constrained perhaps than the farmer. I do not want to get lost in metaphors but merely to indicate my uncertainty on this perennial issue of how much to emphasize agency, or even how much agency is a real issue in analyzing the future of social science.

What I shall do, therefore, is pick a series of cultural prejudices that I think work better than their alternatives and that I hope would serve, in combined form, as the foundation stones of the putatively reconstructed arena I am calling the historical social sciences. Let us start with the very name I am using for this new disciplinary construct. I do not believe that we can talk about the real world in any way that is not based on a claim to science, by which I mean the assumption that the world is real and is potentially knowable (if only perhaps in part). Every word we use in speaking and writing involves a theory and a grand narrative. There is no way to escape this, however much we try or claim we want to escape it. On the other hand, there is no way to analyze or even describe the real world without being historical, by which I mean that the context of any given reality is constantly changing, evolving, and that statements of truth are no longer true the moment after they are uttered. The problem of social science—probably of the natural sciences as well, but I pass on that for the moment—is how to conciliate the search for structural continuities (call them laws or hypotheses if you like) and constant historical change. That is, the problem is to find modes of analysis, or languages, that can bridge this contradiction inherent in the process of knowing.

Stating the issue in this manner is a way of denying the usefulness of the *Methodenstreit,* of rejecting the claims of both nomothetists and idiographers, of saying that we are all condemned to be both things simultaneously and at all times and under all circumstances. Many, even most, present-day social scientists will probably feel quite uncomfortable about this reality, and naturally so, for it violates the cultures within which they have been socialized. But we know that cultures can and do change, that they are malleable, if sometimes with difficulty. And I can hope that fifty years from now at a future Sidney W. Mintz Lecture in Anthropology (although this last term may not survive the transformations), this *Aufhebung* will seem so natural that it will not even be thought necessary to advert to it.

In such a culture, what kind of work shall we be doing? Empirical work, largely, I hope, but of a certain kind. Let me start with what I think is the most pervasive failing of existing social science. Much of what we do is an elaborate explanation of some dependent variable, without any real empirical demonstration that the explicandum is in some sense real. It is all too easy to assume that a credible proposition is a reality. It is against this that Ranke insisted that history must concern itself only with *wie es eigentlich gewesen ist*. And Paul Lazarsfeld long ago (1949) demonstrated that obvious facts are not so obvious once one actually tries to provide evidence for them. And the early ethnographers wrestled with imageries of strange, allegedly savage behavior that seemed to be quite different when seen close at hand. Ranke used his warning to argue that we must search for archival evidence. Lazarsfeld used his warning to argue the utility of public-opinion polling. The ethnographers used their warnings to insist on participant observation. The solutions, it turned out, were many, and all, no doubt, had their limitations. It is the realization of the initial problem that is crucial.

Without a statement about a dependent variable that has been reasonably demonstrated empirically, there can be no analysis. This does not mean that the assertion is correct. There can never be a definitive fact of any kind. But between the definitive fact and the presumed but undemonstrated reality lies a wide range of possibilities, and it is into this murky middle ground—into the world of what has probably really happened in the world—that the historical social sciences are called to work. Deductive models serve us ill. Common knowledge is at best a source of possibly correct perceptions and is itself an object of study. This is why field work (in the loosest, broadest sense of the term) is our eternal responsibility. Once we have something to explain, we need concepts, variables, and methods with which to explain it. And it is about concepts, variables, and methods that we have long been arguing with each other, arguing loudly and on the whole not all that fruitfully.

We all use concepts. How else could we say anything? And we all have a bag of concepts in our minds, ones that we have learned in our continuing education from childhood on. Some of them are as mundane as needs and interests, some as seemingly obvious as society and culture, some as seemingly specific and "advanced" as bourgeoisie and proletariat. They are all challenged by some people, sometimes, but this does not stop others from invoking them. So it is good to remember the admonition of Lucien Febvre (1962, 481), that "it is never a waste of time to write the history of a word." He made this statement when he was writing about the concept of civilization. This elementary truth, largely ignored, is what those devoted to deconstruction have tried to reinvent. We now have a whole *Archiv für Begriffsgeschichte* in Germany, of which I would guess most social scientists are not even aware, or, if they are, ignore on the grounds that these are issues for some specialists—philosophers or historians of ideas.

Nor do most social scientists pay attention to the constraints of morphology. Listing multiple varieties of some phenomenon tends to be a sort of mindless empiricism. Morphologies are ways of creating preliminary order in the "blooming, buzzing confusion" of reality, and in effect are hidden causal hypotheses. They are worth what they are worth, but they tend to be worthless the moment there are too many categories. Usually three or four are the limit. This suggests that social scientists need to examine carefully and repeatedly their philosophical, epistemological premises, and debate them. They do not at present consider *Begriffsgeschichte* or the modes of constructing morphologies a foundation stone of their own research or a necessary part of the pedagogy of graduate education. Here is where their scientism leads to distinctly unscientific outcomes, without even the awareness that this is happening.

As we move from concepts to variables, once again some simple truths are in order. Or, to continue my metaphor, the prejudices of a minority need to be incorporated into the practice of all of us. I want first of all to speak up in favor of the past tense. Virtually all statements should be made in the past tense. To make them in the present tense is to presume universality and eternal reality. The argument should not be made by a grammatical sleight of hand. Anything that happened yesterday is in the past. Generalizations about what happened yesterday are about the past. This is perhaps a sensitive issue for some anthropologists (the famous "anthropological present") and for most mainstream economists and sociologists. But using the past tense serves as a constant reminder of the historicity of our analyses and the necessity for theoretical prudence.

I wish also to make a case for a culture of plurals. Most concepts are plural concepts. Try civilizations, cultures, economies, families, structures of knowledge—the list could go on. It is not that we cannot proffer a definition for a word and insist that what doesn't meet that definition should not be described by that term. But, as we know only too well, almost all conceptual terms are defined in multiple ways, even multitudinous ways, and it is not very helpful to scholarly debate to assume away the debate by deduction from one's definition. Yet much of what we currently do is done in this way, and we are even rewarded for doing this, and quite often penalized for not doing this. Failure to insist on a narrow definition is often pilloried as journalism, eclecticism, or deviation from the truth.

And along with the past tense and plurals comes the culture of multiple temporalities, multiple spatialities, and multiple TimeSpaces. The *Methodenstreit* that has governed most social science since the late nineteenth century has polarized our community into a battleground wherein which we were all adjured to choose one side because the other side was false, or irrelevant, or worse. Not only was this forced conflict counterproductive, but it led us to ignore the existence and importance of other temporalities and spatialities, including, most importantly, Braudel's *longue durée*, the necessary concept if reality is both systemic and historical simultaneously. What we need in our historical social science is to consider what our reality looks like within each of its possible temporalities and spatialities. And this is of course necessary whether we are analyzing a macrotopic like the history of the modern world-system or a microtopic like the introduction of some new element into the life of some remote village.

Whatever our object of investigation, we need a great deal more fluidity in our analyses as we move from one arena to another, from what we like to call the economy to what we like to call the polity to what we like to call the society or the culture. There is no *ceteris paribus,* for the other things are never equal. We may wish to ignore for a moment elements other than the immediate variables we are considering, since we may find it difficult to talk about everything at once. But we can never do this on the assumption that the surrounding variables do not impinge immediately on what we are studying. The whole lesson of the sciences of complexity is that, if one changes the initial conditions ever so minutely, the outcome can be radically different, whatever the truth of the equations we are using.

This leads us, then, to the question of methods and methodologies. In my own education I was taught that there was a radical distinction between what was called, in the jargon of my teachers, small-m methods and big-m methods. Small-m methods are all those practical techniques we use and that in the past were used to define disciplines: simulation, opinion polling, archival research, participant observation, and so on. The only attitude one can take to small-m methods is one of complete catholicity. They are simply methods of estimating, capturing reality. They are worth what they are worth in facing up to the ways in which the world makes it difficult for the researcher to find out anything about the issues in which he or she is interested. Not only are some of these methods not intrinsically better than others, but it is also not true that certain generally described research issues or sites are necessarily and permanently linked with one of these small-m methods. We all need them all. They all have their virtues and their limitations. And graduate students would do well to become acquainted with the widest range of these small-m methods. Since I have been discussing them within the framework of cultural prejudices, I call for setting aside our prejudices. We will be the stronger for it.

But the real question involves big-m methods. For example, should we trust only quantitative or only qualitative data? Here it is not a question of simply being eclectic; it is a question of what kind of data are valid. I myself have some simple rules that seem to me to cull our collective wisdom. It is clear that almost all our statements are quantitative, even when the statements use nothing more than "more" or "important" in their formulations. And it seems to me that it is always more interesting to be quantitatively more exact than to be less exact. Hence, it follows that quantification is desirable whenever it is possible. But that "whenever" encompasses a big caveat. If one makes of serious quantification an imperative and a priority, one risks ending up where the old joke sent us, looking for the lost watch under the lamppost because the light is better there.

But there is more to it than that. We have today a leading mathematician warning us, "The qualitative approach is not a mere stand-in for quantitative methods. It may lead to great theoretical advances, as in fluid dynamics. It has a significant advantage over quantitative methods, namely, stability" (Ekeland 1988, 73). Note well that this goes against one of the main social science arguments for quantification, that of reliability (or stability). And this has to do with what I would call premature quantification. We can only usefully quantify when we are fairly well advanced in the plausibility of our models and the strength of our data. Quantification comes in toward the end of a process, not at the beginning. Indeed, the beginning is preeminently the realm of ethnography and other nonquantitative modes of analysis. These techniques enable us, in a complex situation (and all social situations are complex situations), to tease out the issues and thereby permit us to explore the explanatory connections.

It is qualitative data, not quantitative data, that are simple. Simplicity, however, is not the end goal of the scientific process but rather the starting point. Of course, one can start with simple statistical correlations as well. Complexification is the name of the game. And ever more complex does not at all necessarily mean ever more narrative. It can quite well mean, it might even better mean, more complicated equations, bringing in more and more variables in a controlled fashion.

It is only at this point of relative complexity that we can engage in real comparisons, ones that do not combine the investigated situation of the strange or complicated or exotic with the presumed truth of the situation we think we know well. Arnold Feldman, one of the early sociologists who studied what were in his time called "underdeveloped countries," used to tell the story that, whenever he gave a talk on the patterns he discerned in his work, there was sure to be someone in the audience who would rise and say, "but not in Pago-Pago." It may or may not have been true that what Feldman recounted was not true in Pago-Pago, but what is the relevance of this caution? The critic may have been intending to deny the possibility that patterns exist, or can ever exist. But then why study Pago-Pago? Is it butterfly collecting? Or the critic may have intended to say that Feldman's formulae were too simple, and needed further complexification if they were to be useful. Or perhaps the critic merely felt that the organizers should have invited him to lecture rather than Feldman. Criticism is a crucial tool within the historical social sciences, but not mindless criticism.

And that brings me to narratives. Who does not like narratives? Narratives are an admirably understandable and attractive way of communicating perceptions of reality. To be sure, even the harshest set of differential equations are a form of narrative, though not the most palatable form. There have been many attacks of late on macronarratives by other narrators. I suppose these persons think that what they do are micronarratives, and that micro is better than macro. But of course micro is a setting in which macro displays itself and which can never be understood without reference to the macro setting. In the end all narratives are macronarratives. The only question is whether we are putting forward a defensible macronarrative.

The culture of the historical social sciences that I envisage will not be against theorizing or theories, but it will be cautious about premature closures. Indeed, the breadth of data, of methods, of linkages to the rest of the world of knowledge would be its principal characteristic. Vigorous analysis within a climate of tolerant and skeptical debate would be what would aid it most. Of course, I am also assuming that in the next fifty years we shall be overcoming the relatively recent (only two centuries old) but deeply rooted divorce between philosophy and science—the so-called two cultures—and that we shall be setting out on the path of constructing a singular epistemology for all knowledge. In this scenario, a reinvigorated social science, one that is both structural and historical, can provide the crucial link between the domains we today classify as the natural sciences and those we classify as the humanities.

The adventure of the historical social sciences is still in its infancy. The possibilities of enabling us to make substantively rational choices in an intrinsically uncertain world lie before us and give us cause for hope amid what are now the gloomy times of a historical transition from our world-system to the next one, a transition that is occurring necessarily in the structures of knowledge as well. Let us at least try seriously to mend our collective ways and to search for more useful paths. Let us make our disciplines less dubious.

Acknowledgments

Chapter 1, "For Science, Against Scientism: The Dilemmas of Contemporary Knowledge Production," reproduced from Partha Nath Mukherji, ed., *Methodology in Social Research: Dilemmas and Perspectives*, 87–92. Copyright © Partha Nath Mukherji 2000. All rights reserved. Reproduced with the permission of the copyright-holder and the publishers, Sage Publications India Pvt. Ltd., New Delhi, India.

Chapter 2, "Social Sciences in the Twenty-first Century," Ali Kazancigil and D. Makinson, eds., *World Social Science Report, 1999*, 42–49. © 1999 UNESCO, reproduced by permission of UNESCO.

Chapter 3, "The End of Certainties in the Social Sciences," *Scienza e Storia*, no. 13, 2000: 17–29. Courtesy of Giampiero Bozzolato, CISST.

Chapter 4, "Braudel and Interscience: A Preacher to Empty Pews?" *Review* 24, no. 1, 2001: 3–12. Courtesy of *Review*.

Chapter 5, "Time and Duration: The Unexcluded Middle, or Reflections on Braudel and Prigogine," reprinted by permission of Sage Publications Ltd. from "Time and Duration: The Unexcluded Middle," *Thesis Eleven* 54, no. 1, 1998. Copyright © Sage Publications Ltd. and Thesis Eleven Pty. Ltd., 1998.

Chapter 6, "The Itinerary of World-Systems Analysis, or How to Resist Becoming a Theory," J. Berger and M. Zelditch Jr., eds., *New Directions in Contemporary Sociological Theory*, 358–76.

Lanham, Md.: Rowman & Littlefield, 2002. Courtesy of The Rowman & Littlefield Publishing Group.

Chapter 7, "History in Search of Science," *Review* 19, no. 1, winter 1996: 11–22. Courtesy of *Review.*

Chapter 8, "Writing History," J. Denolf and B. Simons, eds., *(Re)constructing the Past/Het Verleden als Instrument/Le Passé Composé,* 381–93. Brussels: Carl de Keyser/Magnum, 2000. Courtesy of Carl de Keyser/Magnum.

Chapter 9, "Global Culture(s): Salvation, Menace, or Myth?" C.-H. Hauptmeyer et al., eds., *Die Welt Querdenken,* Festschrift for Hans-Heinrich Nolte. Frankfurt: Peter Lang, 2003. Courtesy of Peter Lang GmbH.

Chapter 10, "From Sociology to Historical Social Science: Prospects and Obstacles," *British Journal of Sociology,* Millennium issue, 51, no. 1, Jan.–Mar. 2000: 25–35. First published in the *British Journal of Sociology* by Routledge Ltd. on behalf of the London School of Economics. © The London School of Economics and Political Science, 2000.

Chapter 11, "Anthropology, Sociology, and Other Dubious Disciplines," *Current Anthropology* 44, no. 4, Aug.–Oct. 2003. © 2003 by the Wenner-Gren Foundation for Anthropological Research. All rights reserved.

Notes

Chapter Two

1. Walter Rüegg (1966, 18) reminds us: "The problem of the 'two cultures' did not exist in the universities before the eighteenth century. Immanuel Kant (1724–1804) could have become a professor of poetry; he delivered lectures over the whole range of the human sciences from pedagogy, anthropology and natural law, to the various fields of philosophy, to geography, mathematics and astronomy. His first groundbreaking works of 1755 were devoted to the emergence of the astronomical system."

2. By 1781 a new university in Stuttgart had eliminated philosophy and theology altogether and added to medicine and law the faculties of military science, *Cameralwissenschaft* (public administration), forestry, and economics. When the French universities were abolished during the French Revolution, all that was left were the specialized schools outside the university, which Napoleon used as the basis of the *Grandes Ecoles*. See Frijhoff 1996, 46, 57–58; see also Hammerstein 1996, 633.

3. Because of this, many scientific institutions were at first created outside the universities. It was "only in the eighteenth century [that the exact sciences were] allowed their due place in university teaching *stricto sensu*, . . . and only much later by the foundation of true faculties of science" (Frijhoff 1996, 57). Roy Porter (1996) asserts that this is somewhat overstated, essentially arguing that scientific knowledge was being purveyed within the university systems in the seventeenth and eighteenth centuries, but *sub rosa*. However, even he admits that the situation was not one of full integration.

4. For a bibliographical overview of the field as of 1992, see Lee 1992.

5. There is, virtually by definition, no canonical overview of cultural studies. For one omnibus collection, see Grossberg, Nelson, and Treichler 1992.

Chapter Six

1. My master's thesis in 1954 was entitled "McCarthyism and the Conservative." My Ph.D. dissertation in 1959 was entitled "The Role of Voluntary Associations in the Nationalist Movements in Ghana and the Ivory Coast." It was later published as *The Road to Independence: Ghana and the Ivory Coast* (1964). At the first ISA meeting that I attended in Stresa, Italy, in 1959, I spent my time at the meetings of the Committee on Political Sociology. Later I attended one of the conferences of the SSRC Committee in Frascati, Italy, in 1964, and contributed a paper to the volume resulting from the conference: "The Decline of the Party in Single-Party African States" (1966).

2. See my look backward as of 2000 (Wallerstein 2000a).

3. My first two books, aside from the published dissertation, were *Africa: The Politics of Independence* (1961) and *Africa: The Politics of Unity* (1965). In 1973–74, I was elected president of the African Studies Association.

4. *La Méditerranée et le monde méditerranéen à l'époque de Philippe II* was first published in 1949; a revised edition in two volumes appeared in 1966. The English translation, based on the revised version, *The Mediterranean and the Mediterranean World in the Age of Philip II,* did not appear until 1972.

5. I acknowledged my debt to both of them in Wallerstein 1974a, xi.

6. Note the hyphen in all of these formulations. "World empire" (and *Weltreich*) is a term that others have used before me. I felt, however, that since none of these structures was global, in English the hyphen was required by the same grammatical logic that made it requisite in the case of world-economy.

7. By now Frank has published these arguments in many texts. See especially the early version (1990) and the mature version (1999). For my critique of *ReOrient,* see Wallerstein 1999 and the other critical reviews of Frank by Samir Amin and Giovanni Arrighi in the same issue of *Review.*

8. I discussed how best to translate them into English in Wallerstein 1988b.

9. See, for example, Hechter, who tempered his praise with a critique of shortcomings, two of which revolve around theorizing. "[T]he is no theory to account for the triumph of the European world-economy in the sixteenth century. . . . There is a certain lack of conceptual precision which mars the analysis" (1975, 221).

10. See the marvelous discussion of the criticism that Wallerstein has "only one case" in Wulbert 1975.

11. One of the few persons to remark favorably upon this technique, and to explicate clearly the strategy, was Franco Moretti (2000, 56–57): "Writing about comparative social history, Marc Bloch once coined a lovely 'slogan', as he himself called it: 'years of analysis for a day of synthesis'; and if you read Braudel or Wallerstein you immediately see what Bloch had in mind. The text which is strictly Wallerstein's, his 'day of synthesis', occupies one third of a page, one fourth, maybe half; the rest are quotations (fourteen hundred, in the first volume of *The Modern World-System*). Years of analysis; other people's analysis, which Wallerstein synthesizes into a system."

12. "Is there good reason for considering Poland part of the periphery within Europe's world-economy and regarding the Ottoman empire as part of an external arena?" (Lane 1976, 528).

13. "Thus the correct counterposition cannot be production for the market versus production for use, but the class system of production based on free wage labour (capitalism) versus pre-capitalist class systems" (Brenner 1977, 50).

14. Theda Skocpol, like Brenner, who acknowledged seeing her article before publication, suggested that I ignored the "basic Marxist insight that the social relations of production and surplus appropriation are the sociological key to the functioning and development of any economic system" (1977, 1079). However, her more fundamental critique had to do with the relation of the economic and political arenas: "[The] model is based on a two-step reduction: first, a reduction of socio-economic structure to determination by world market opportunities and technological production possibilities; and second, a reduction of state structures and policies to determination by dominant class interests" (1078–79). Aristide Zolberg, in his 1981 critique of my work, specifically recommended Hintze as a more "fruitful avenue for theoretical reflection." He said that Hintze "remains one of the very few scholars who identify the interactions between endogenous processes of various kinds and exogenous *political* processes as a *problématique* for the analysis of European political development" (278). Note the italicization of "political." For Zolberg, as for Skocpol, as indeed for Brenner, I am too "economistic."

15. Core-periphery as an antinomy to be applied to the analysis of the world-economy was first made famous by Raúl Prebisch and his associates in the UN Economic Commission of Latin America in the 1950s, essentially to replace the then-dominant antinomy of industrialized and agricultural nations. Prebisch was implicitly using a world-systems perspective by insisting that what went on in the two sets of countries was a function of their interrelations more than of social structures internal to

each set of countries. The Prebisch framework was further developed, particularly in its political implications, by what came to be known in the 1960s as dependency theory. In volume 1 of *The Modern World-System*, I insisted on adding a third category, the semiperiphery, which I claimed was not merely in between the other two but played a crucial role in making the system work. What the semiperiphery is, and how exactly it can be defined, has been a contentious issue ever since. I made an early attempt to spell this out in Wallerstein 1976b.

16. See the web site http://fbc.binghamton.edu.

17. See my discussion of this issue, precisely using the case of Germany to make a general theoretical point, in "Societal Development, or Development of the World-System?" This was an address to the *Deutsche Soziologentag* and was first published in 1986.

18. I have discussed a bit of this organizational history and philosophy in Wallerstein 1998a.

19. The story from 1976 to 1991 can be found in a pamphlet entitled *Report on an Intellectual Project: The Fernand Braudel Center, 1976–1991* (Wallerstein 1991a). It is now out of print but can be found on the web at http://fbc.binghamton.edu/fbcintel.htm. The annual story since then can be found in the newsletters of the FBC, also on the web at http://fbc.binghamton.edu/newsletter.htm.

20. See Aronowitz 1981. The bulk of the article attacked the uses of "systems theory" for its nomothetic bias, and then drew this inference: "Ideologies of legitimation, questions of cultural domination, etc. take on little or no importance. . . . Wallerstein sees no need to account for the specific development of hegemonic bourgeois democratic ideologies which are already in the process of formation in the period of capitalism's early rise" (516).

21. "[O]ur position is that classical mechanics is incomplete, because it does not include irreversible processes associated with an increase in entropy. To include these processes in its formulation, we must incorporate instability and nonintegrability. Integrable systems are the exception. Starting with the three-body problem, most dynamical systems are nonintegrable. . . . We therefore obtain a probabilistic formulation of dynamics by means of which we can resolve the conflict between time-reversible dynamics and the time-oriented view of thermodynamics" (Prigogine 1997, 108).

22. The latest and clearest version is to be found in *The End of Certainty* (Prigogine 1997). It should be noted that even here the issues of orthography intrude themselves. "Certainty," in the English edition, is singular. But the French original is entitled *La fin des certitudes*, and there "cer-

tainty" is plural. I believe the publishers made a serious error in the translation of the title.

23. On the importance of "unthinking" as opposed to "rethinking," see Wallerstein 2001, 1–4 and passim.

24. I placed the discussion of "free will" within a fifth social time, not dealt with by Braudel. I called it "transformational time" and suggested that this was the *kairos* discussed by Paul Tillich (1948, esp. 32–51). *Kairos* means "the right time" and Tillich said that "All great changes in history are accompanied by a strong consciousness of a kairos at hand" (155). See Wallerstein 1988a, 296, where I specifically tied the concept of transformational time to Prigogine's discussion of the consequences of "cascading bifurcations."

25. The six vectors are the interstate system, world production, the world labor force, world human welfare, the social cohesion of the states, and structures of knowledge. These six vectors are then summed up in two chapters I wrote for *The Age of Transition* (Hopkins and Wallerstein 1996), entitled "The Global Picture, 1945–1990" and "The Global Possibilities, 1990–2025."

26. The importance of the time dimension in the redirecting of sociological theorizing is at the heart of my ISA presidential address (Wallerstein 1999).

27. The final list of the commission was Immanuel Wallerstein, chair, sociology, U.S.; Calestous Juma, science and technology studies, Kenya; Evelyn Fox Keller, physics, U.S.; Jürgen Kocka, history, Germany; Dominique Lecourt, philosophy, France; V. Y. Mudimbe, romance languages, Congo; Kinhide Mushakoji, political science, Japan; Ilya Prigogine, chemistry, Belgium; Peter J. Taylor, geography, U.K., Michel-Rolph Trouillot, anthropology, Haiti. Given the academic and geographic mobility of scholars, the disciplines listed are those in which they received their doctorates, and the countries those of their identification (via birth or nationality).

28. As of 2003 the report existed in twenty-seven editions in twenty-four languages. Others are in process.

Chapter Nine

1. The United Nations proclaimed in 1948 a Universal Declaration of Human Rights.

2. See the acerbic comments of Alex de Waal (2001, 15): "So the global principle now extends far enough to take care of war criminals hostile to the US."

3. This is what Oren Yiftachel (2001, 2) suggests Ella Shohat is doing. Shohat herself is concerned with the assertion of a "Mizrahi identity" against the Zionist construction of a "Jewish nation." She says: "[I]magining an intellectual space for critical Mizrahi work necessitates the pluralization and de-essentialization of *all* identities." She goes on to insist: "The concept of relationality that I am calling for should not be confused with cultural relativism. Although the concept of relationality goes back to structuralism and post-structuralism, I have also been using the term in a trans-linguistic, dialogic, and historicized sense. The project of a relational multicultural analysis has to be situated historically and geographically as a set of contested practices" (2001, 89–91).

4. See the report on the findings of a group of astrophysicists, reported in the *New York Times*, Aug. 15, 2001, which revealed that at least one presumed "constant of nature"—fine structure constant—turns out not in fact to be constant.

Chapter Ten

1. Weber 1968, 85–86. I discuss Weber's usage and the issue in general in Wallerstein 1996.

Chapter Eleven

1. Mintz 1978. Mintz inserted an opening footnote: "I am grateful to Professor Wallerstein for the opportunity to air my views and, indeed, for the choice of topic, to which he asked me to address myself."

2. Michel-Rolph Trouillot was the anthropologist member of this commission.

References

Amin, Samir. 1999. History conceived as an eternal cycle. *Review* 22 (3): 291–326.

Aronowitz, Stanley. 1981. A metatheoretical critique of Immanuel Wallerstein's *The modern world-system*. *Theory and Society* 10 (July): 503–20.

Arrighi, Giovanni. 1999. The world according to Andre Gunder Frank. *Review* 22 (3): 327–54.

Bell, David A. 2002. He wouldn't dare. *London Review of Books*. May 9: 19.

Bourdieu, Pierre. 1975. La spécificité du champ scientifique et les conditions sociales du progrès de la raison. *Sociologie et société* 3 (May): 91–118.

Braudel, Fernand. 1949. *La Méditerranée et le monde méditerranéen à l'époque de Philippe II*. Paris: Armand Colin.

———. 1966. *La Méditerranée et le monde méditerranéen à l'époque de Philippe II*. Rev. and enl. ed. 2 vols. Paris: Lib. Armand Colin.

———. 1969a. Histoire et sciences sociales: La longue durée. In Fernand Braudel, *Ecrits sur l'histoire*, 41–83. Paris: Flammarion. First published in *Annales E.S.C.* 13 (Oct.–Dec. 1958): 725–53.

———. 1969b. Unité et diversité des sciences de l'homme. In Fernand Braudel, *Ecrits sur l'histoire*, 85–96. Paris: Flammarion. First published in *Revue de l'enseignement supérieur*, no. 1 (1960): 17–22.

———. 1969c. Histoire et sociologie. In Fernand Braudel, *Ecrits sur l'histoire*, 97–122. Paris: Flammarion. First published as chap. 4 of *Traité de sociologie*, edited by Georges Gurvitch. Paris: Presses Universitaires de France, 2 vols. (1958–60).

———. 1972. *The Mediterranean and the Mediterranean world in the age of Philip II*. New York: Harper & Row.

———. 1984a. *Civilization and capitalism, 15th–18th century*. Vol. 3, *The perspective of the world*. New York: Harper & Row.

———. 1984b. Une vie pour l'histoire. *Magazin Littéraire*, no. 212 (November): 18–24.

Brenner, Robert. 1977. The origins of capitalist development: A critique of neo-Smithian Marxism. *New Left Review* 104 (July–Aug.): 23–92.

Chaunu, Pierre. 1973. *L'Espagne de Charles Quint*. Part 1. Paris: S.E.D.E.S.

Darnton, Robert. 1999. History lessons. *Perspectives* (American Historical Association) (September): 2–3.

De Waal, Alex. 2001. The moral solipsism of global ethics inc. *London Review of Books* 23 (Aug. 23): 15.

Diamond, Sigmund. 1992. *Compromised campus: The collaboration of universities with the intelligence community, 1945–1955*. New York: Oxford Univ. Press.

Dreifus, Claudia. 2002. Finding rich fodder in nuclear scientists. *New York Times*. May 21.

Ekeland, Ivar. 1988. *Mathematics and the unexpected*. Chicago: Univ. of Chicago Press.

Febvre, Lucien. 1962. Civilisation: Évolution d'un mot et d'un groupe d'idées. In *Pour une histoire à part entière*, 481–528. Paris: SEVPEN.

Frank, Andre Gunder. 1990. A theoretical introduction to 5000 years of world system history. *Review* 13: 155–248.

———. 1999. *ReOrient: Global economy in the Asian age*. Berkeley: University of California Press.

Frijhoff, Willem. 1996. Patterns. In *Universities in early modern Europe (1500–1800)*. Vol. 2 of *A history of the university in Europe*, ed. H. de Ridder-Symoens, 43–110. Cambridge: Cambridge Univ. Press.

Grossberg, Lawrence, Cary Nelson, and Paula Treichler, eds. 1992. *Cultural studies*. New York: Routledge.

Hammerstein, Notker. 1996. Epilogue: The Enlightenment. In *Universities in early modern Europe (1500–1800)*. Vol. 2 of *A history of the university in Europe*, ed. H. de Ridder-Symoens, 621–40. Cambridge: Cambridge Univ. Press.

Hechter, Michael. 1975. Review of *The modern world-system*, by Immanuel Wallerstein. *Contemporary Sociology* 4 (3): 217–22.

Hopkins, Terence K., and Immanuel Wallerstein. 1967. The comparative study of national societies. *Social Science Information* 6 (Oct.): 25–58.

———, coords. 1996. *The age of transition*. London: Zed Press.

Jeanneret, Yves. 1998. *L'affaire Sokal ou la querelle des impostures*. Paris: Presses Univ. de France.

Lambropoulos, Vassilis. 1993. *The rise of Eurocentrism: Anatomy of interpretation*. Princeton: Princeton Univ. Press.

Lane, Frederic. 1976. Economic growth in Wallerstein's social system. *Comparative Studies in Society and History* 18 (Oct.): 577–82.

Lazarsfeld, Paul F. 1949. "The American soldier": An expository review. *Public Opinion Quarterly* 13 (3): 377–404.

Lee, Richard. 1992. Readings in the "new science": A selective annotated bibliography. *Review* 15 (winter): 113–71.

———. 1996. Structures of knowledge. In *The age of transition,* coord. Terence K. Hopkins and Immanuel Wallerstein, 178–206. London: Zed Press.

Lingua Franca. 2000. *The Sokal hoax: The sham that shook the academy.* Lincoln: Univ. of Nebraska Press.

Lyon, Bryce, and Mary Lyon. 1991. *The birth of Annales history: The letters of Lucien Febvre and Marc Bloch to Henri Pirenne (1921–1935).* Brussels: Académie Royale de Belgique, Commission Royale.

Małowist, Marian. 1964. Les aspects sociaux de la première phase de l'expansion coloniale. *Africana Bulletin* 1: 11–40.

———. 1966. Le commerce d'or et d'esclaves au Soudan occidental. *Africana Bulletin* 4: 49–93.

Merton, Robert K. 1957. The bearing of sociological theory on empirical research. In *Social theory and social structure,* rev. and enl. ed. Glencoe, Ill.: Free Press.

Mintz, Sidney. 1978. Was the plantation slave a proletarian? *Review* 2 (summer): 81–98.

Moretti, Franco. 2000. Conjectures on world literature. *New Left Review,* 2d series, no. 1 (Jan.–Feb.): 5–24.

Nolte, H. H. 1982. The position of Eastern Europe in the international system in early modern times. *Review* 6 (summer): 25–84.

Novick, Peter. 1988. *That noble dream: The "objectivity question" and the American historical profession.* Cambridge: Cambridge Univ. Press.

Pirenne, Henri. 1931. La tâche de l'historien. *Le Flambeau* 14, 5–22. English-language version in *Methods in Social Science: A Case Book,* ed. Stuart A. Rice, 435–45. Chicago: Univ. of Chicago Press, 1931.

Polanyi, Karl. 1957. *The great transformation.* Boston: Beacon Press.

———. 1967. The economy as instituted process. In *Trade and Market in the Early Empires,* ed. K. Polanyi et al., 243–70. Glencoe, Ill.: Free Press.

———. 1977. Forms of integration and supporting structures. In Karl Polanyi, *The livelihood of man,* ed. Harry W. Pearson, 35–43. New York: Academic Press.

Pollock, Sheldon. 1993. Deep Orientalism? Notes on Sanskrit and power behind the Raj. In *Orientalism and the postcolonial predicament,* ed. C. A. Breckenridge and P. van der Veer, 76–133. Philadelphia: Univ. of Pennsylvania Press.

Porter, Roy. 1996. The scientific revolution and universities. In *Universities in early modern Europe (1500–1800).* Vol. 2 of *A history of the university in Europe,* ed. H. de Ridder-Symoens, 531–62. Cambridge: Cambridge Univ. Press.

Prigogine, Ilya. 1997. *The end of certainty: Time, chaos and the laws of nature.* New York: Free Press.

Prigogine, Ilya, and Isabelle Stengers. 1979. *La nouvelle alliance.* Paris: Gallimard.

Rüegg, Walter. 1996. Foreword. In *Universities in early modern Europe (1500–1800).* Vol. 2 of *A history of the university in Europe,* ed. H. de Ridder-Symoens, xix–xxiii. Cambridge: Cambridge Univ. Press.

Sachs, Justice Albie. 1998. Fourth D. T. Lakdawala memorial lecture, given at Institute of Social Sciences, Nehru Memorial Museum and Library Auditorium, New Delhi, Dec. 18.

Santos, Boaventura de Sousa. 1992. A discourse on the sciences. *Review* 15 (winter): 9–47.

Shapin, Steven. 1994. *A social history of truth: Civility and science in seventeenth-century England.* Chicago: Univ. of Chicago Press.

Shohat, Ella (2001). Rupture and return: The shaping of a Mizrahi epistemology. *Hagar* 2 (1): 61–92.

Skocpol Theda. 1977. Wallerstein's world capitalist system: A theoretical and historical critique. *American Journal of Sociology* 82 (May): 1075–89.

Snow, C. P. 1965. *The two cultures, and a second look.* 2d ed. Cambridge: Cambridge Univ. Press.

Stengers, Isabelle. 1996. *Cosmopolitique I: La guerre des sciences.* Paris: La Découverte.

Tillich, Paul. 1948. *The Protestant era.* Chicago: Univ. of Chicago Press.

Truth and Reconciliation Commission (South Africa). 1999. *Truth and Reconciliation Commission of South Africa Report.* Cape Town: Truth and Reconciliation Commission.

Wallerstein, Immanuel. 1961. *Africa: The politics of independence.* New York: Random House.

———. 1964. *The road to independence: Ghana and the Ivory Coast.* Paris: Mouton.

———. 1965. *Africa: The politics of unity.* New York: Random House.

———. 1966. The decline of the party in single-party African states. In *Political Parties and Political Development,* ed. J. LaPalombara and M. Weiner, 201–14. Princeton: Princeton Univ. Press.

———. 1967. The comparative study of national societies. *Social Science Information* 6 (Oct.): 25–58.

———. 1968. Frantz Fanon. In *International encyclopedia of the social sciences* 5:326–27.

———. 1970. Frantz Fanon: Reason and violence. *Berkeley Journal of Sociology* 15: 222–31.

———. 1974a. *The modern world-system*. Vol. 1, *Capitalist agriculture and the origins of the European world-economy in the sixteenth century*. New York: Academic Press.

———. 1974b. The rise and demise of the world-capitalist system: Concepts for comparative analysis. *Comparative Studies in Society and History* 16 (Sept.): 387–415. Reprinted in *The capitalist world-economy*, 1–36. Cambridge: Cambridge Univ. Press, 1979.

———. 1976a. Modernization: Requiescat in pace. In *The uses and controversy of sociology*, ed. L. Coser and O. Larsen, 131–35. New York: Free Press. Reprinted in *The capitalist world-economy*, 132–37. Cambridge: Cambridge Univ. Press, 1979.

———. 1976b. Semiperipheral countries and the contemporary world crisis. *Theory and Society* 3 (winter): 461–83. Reprinted in *The capitalist world-economy*, 95–118. Cambridge: Cambridge Univ. Press, 1979.

———. 1978. Civilizations and modes of production: Conflicts and convergences. *Theory and Society* 5: 1–10. Reprinted in *Politics of the world-economy*, 159–68. Cambridge: Cambridge Univ. Press, 1984.

———. 1979. Fanon and the revolutionary class. In *The capitalist world-economy*, 250–68. Cambridge: Cambridge Univ. Press, 1979.

———. 1986. Societal development, or development of the world-system? *International Sociology* 1 (Mar.): 1–17. Reprinted in *The essential Wallerstein*, 112–28. New York: New Press, 2000.

———. 1987. World-systems analysis. In *Social theory today*, ed. A. Giddens and J. Turner, 309–24. Cambridge: Polity Press. Reprinted as Call for a debate about the paradigm, in *Unthinking social science: The limits of nineteenth-century paradigms*, 2d ed., 237–56. Philadelphia: Temple Univ. Press, 2001.

———. 1988a. What can one mean by southern culture? In *The evolution of southern culture*, ed. N. M. Bartley, 1–13. Athens: Univ. of Georgia Press.

———. 1988b. The invention of TimeSpace realities: Towards an understanding of our historical systems. *Geography* 73 (Oct.). Reprinted in *Unthinking social science: The limits of nineteenth-century paradigms*, 2d ed., 135–48. Philadelphia: Temple Univ. Press, 2001.

———. 1989. Culture as the ideological battleground of the modern world-system. *Hitotsubashi Journal of Social Studies* 21 (Aug.): 5–22. Reprinted in *The essential Wallerstein*, 264–89. New York: New Press, 2000.

———. 1990a. Culture is the world-system: A reply to Boyne. *Theory, Culture, and Society* 7 (June): 63–65.

———. 1990b. World-systems analysis: The second phase. *Review* 13 (spring): 287–93. Reprinted in *The end of the world as we know it: Social science for the twenty-first century*, 192–201. Minneapolis: Univ. of Minnesota Press, 1999.

———. 1991a. *Report on an intellectual project: The Fernand Braudel center, 1976–1991*. Binghamton, N.Y.: Fernand Braudel Center.

———. 1991b. World system versus world-systems: A critique. *Critique of Anthropology* 11 (2): 189–94.

———. 1993a. The geoculture of development, or the transformation of our geoculture? *Asian Perspective* 17 (fall–winter): 211–25. Reprinted in *After liberalism*, 162–75. New York: New Press, 1995.

———. 1993b. The TimeSpace of world-systems analysis: A philosophical essay. *Historical Geography* 23 (1–2): 5–22.

———. 1994. Peace, stability, and legitimacy, 1990–2025/2050. In *The fall of great powers*, ed. Geir Lundestad, 331–49. Oslo: Scandinavian Univ. Press. Reprinted in *The essential Wallerstein*, 435–53. New York: New Press, 2000.

———. 1995a. *After liberalism*. New York: New Press.

———. 1995b. *Historical capitalism, with capitalist civilization*. London: Verso.

———. 1995c. The significance of political sociology. In *Encounter with Erik Allardt*, ed. R. Alapuro et al., 27–28. Helsinki: Yliopistopaino.

———. 1995d. What do we bound, and whom, when we bound social research? *Social Research* 62 (winter): 839–56. Reprinted in *The essential Wallerstein*, 170–84. New York: New Press, 2000.

———. 1996. Social science and contemporary society: The vanishing guarantees of rationality. *International Sociology* 11 (Mar.): 7–26. Reprinted in *The end of the world as we know it: Social science for the twenty-first century*, 137–56. Minneapolis: Univ. of Minnesota Press, 1999.

———. 1997a. The national and the universal: Can there be such a thing as world culture? In *Culture, globalization, and the world-system*, ed. A. D. King, 91–105. Minneapolis: Univ. of Minnesota Press.

———. 1997b. The unintended consequences of cold war area studies. In *The cold war and the university: Toward an intellectual history of the postwar years*, N. Chomsky et al., 195–231. New York: New Press.

———. 1998a. Pedagogy and scholarship. In *Mentoring, methods, and movements: Colloquium in honor of Terence K. Hopkins by his former students*, ed. I. Wallerstein, 47–52. Binghamton, N.Y.: Fernand Braudel Center.

———. 1998b. *Utopistics: or, historical choices for the twenty-first century*. New York: New Press.

———. 1999. The heritage of sociology, the promise of social science. *Current Sociology* 47 (Jan.): 1–37. Reprinted in *The end of the world as we know it: Social science for the twenty-first century*, 220–51. Minneapolis: Univ. of Minnesota Press, 1999.

———. 2000a. C'était quoi, le tiers-monde? *Le monde diplomatique* (Aug.): 18–19.

———. 2000b. From sociology to historical social science: Prospects and obstacles. *British Journal of Sociology* 51 (Jan.–Mar.): 25–35.

———. 2000c. Globalization or the age of transition?: A long-term view of the trajectory of the world-system. *International Sociology* 15 (June): 249–65. Reprinted in *Decline of American power: The U.S. in a chaotic world*, 45–68. New York: New Press, 2003.

———. 2001. *Unthinking social science: The limits of nineteenth-century paradigms,* 2d ed. Philadelphia: Temple Univ. Press.

———. 2003. Who are we? Who are the others? In *Decline of American power: The U.S. in a chaotic world,* 124–48. New York: New Press, 2003.

Wallerstein, Immanuel, et al. 1996. *Open the social sciences: Report of the Gulbenkian commission on the reconstruction of the social sciences.* Stanford: Stanford Univ. Press.

Weber, Max. 1946. *From Max Weber: Essays in sociology.* New York: Oxford Univ. Press.

———. 1968. *Economy and society.* New York: Bedminster.

Whitehead, Alfred North. 1948. *Science and the modern world.* New York: Mentor.

Wulbert, Roland. 1975. Had by the positive integer. *American Sociologist* 10 (Nov.): 243.

Yiftachel, Oren. 2001. Inequalities: Fate or state? *Hagar* 2 (1): 1–3.

Zolberg, Aristide. 1981. The origins of the modern world-system: A missing link. *World Politics* 33 (Jan.): 253–81.

Index

The entire book is about the uncertainties of knowledge and the epistemological divide between science and philosophy (or the humanities). It therefore seems pointless to index the terms "knowledge" (certain or uncertain), "science" (or faculty of sciences), or "philosophy" (or faculty of philosophy or humanities).

All of the terms in this index are listed as nouns. Whenever they are used as adjectives or noun variants, they are included in the listing.

207

Immanuel Wallerstein is Director of the Fernand Braudel Center, Binghamton University, and Senior Research Scholar at Yale University.